AMBUSHED AND OUTNUMBERED. HE MUST SET THE EXAMPLE THEY WILL FOLLOW.

As he moved along the line a stream of machine-gun fire started to pour in from the right flank killing several of the innate Vietnamese soldiers. Davis made his way quickly toward the flank and came face to face with five Vietcong climbing over the shallow ditch. A scathing burst from his M-16 killed all five and he returned to the center of the ditch line after persuading two of his terrified soldiers to guard the right flank.

As he was moving back to the center of the defensive line he heard a burst of automatic rifle fire coming from the left flank and he made his way rapidly toward it. The soldiers on the left flank were huddled down behind a small ditch, rigid with fear. Six Vietcong were moving quickly toward the position and Davis pulled the pin from a fragmentation grenade and hurled it in their midst. The explosion felled four of the enemy but the remaining pair continued their charge. Davis leveled his M-16 and squeezed the trigger. The result was a dull click instead of the powerful crack he expected. His immediate reaction was to change the magazine but as soon as he removed the one on the weapon he realized it was not empty—the gun had jammed!

Bantam Books in The Fighting Elite series

U.S. MARINES
U.S. RANGERS
U.S. NAVY SEALS
U.S. AIR COMMANDO
U.S. ARMY SPECIAL FORCES
U.S. MARINE AIRWINGS (Forthcoming)

The Fighting Elite ™
U.S. ARMY SPECIAL FORCES
Ian Padden

BANTAM BOOKS
TORONTO • NEW YORK • LONDON • SYDNEY • AUCKLAND

THE FIGHTING ELITE™: U.S. ARMY SPECIAL FORCES

A Bantam Book / January 1985

*Produced by Bruck Communications, Inc.
157 West 57th Street, New York, NY 10019.*

*Cover photo courtesy U.S. Army
Inside photos courtesy D.A.V.A.*

ISBN 0-553-25358-1

Published simultaneously in the United States and Canada

PRINTED IN THE UNITED STATES OF AMERICA

H   0 9 8 7 6 5 4 3 2 1

To Morgan Cresswell
In memory of the hell we
went through during
"Operation Sidi Barrani"

And to Faris Whitley, a superb warrior who risked his
life alongside me in a dark and dangerous world.

Acknowledgments

Many thanks to the Department of the Army; the Department of State; the Public Affairs Office, U.S. Army Special Warfare Center; Captain Michael A. Phillips, U.S. Army Special Warfare Center, Fort Bragg, North Carolina; the staff of the Defense Audio Visual Aid Department, Washington, D.C.; Lieutenant Colonel Sully Fontaine, USASF retired; Major Herbert Brucker, USASF retired; Major Richard D. Bishop, USASF retired; and the United States Army Special Forces Association.

Contents

Foreword

When a war or a battle is mentioned, most people think of opposing armies facing each other from opposite sides of a well-defined front line. It is assumed that each army is intent upon pushing the other back or destroying it in order to occupy territory.

When nations engage in war—on land, at sea, or in the air—if there is a definite separation, or front line, with each force in control of the territory that it occupies, it is generally called *conventional* warfare.

However, during any conventional war there are often tactical requirements that necessitate raids or excursions behind the enemy's front lines. These are usually carried out for the purposes of disrupting lines of communications and supplies, gathering intelligence information, rescuing friendly agents or downed pilots, or simple harassment to confuse the enemy.

This kind of operation falls under the heading of *unconventional*, or special, warfare. And, as well as requiring a very different tactical approach from that of conventional warfare, it requires specialized equipment and uniquely trained personnel.

Another form of unconventional warfare—perhaps the most modern—which has become prevalent in the past twenty years, is *insurgency*.

Insurgency exploits the political, social, and economic difficulties of a country in order to create strife and turmoil within the nation; the primary purpose of this exploitation is to gain the people's support and sympathy for the insurgents' belief or cause. The methods employed are psychological and extremely subversive in nature, and they work equally well in both the so-called primitive and the advanced nations. However, success in the primitive nations is usually achieved more rapidly.

Guerrilla warfare is the oldest form of unconventional warfare. It is as old as war itself and was originally employed in conjunction with conventional armies. But in recent times the guerrilla has taken on a new role: he has become both the violent weapon of insurgency and the physical tool of revolutionary movements for achieving political power.

During the past twenty years, the rise of insurgency and the success of guerrilla warfare against well-trained and well-armed conventional armies throughout the world has posed a growing threat to the objectives of the United States. The inability of conventional forces to handle both the guerrilla and the insurgent has been clearly demonstrated on numerous occasions in recent years. As a result, the United States government directed our military leaders to organize and train special units, within the existing defense structure, in the disciplines and tactics required to counter the growing threat.

The Army Special Forces is one of these units. Its formation, structure, training, and deployment are designed to counter the threat based on the following Army definitions:

Unconventional Warfare: "The three interrelated fields of guerrilla warfare, evasion and escape, and subversion against hostile states."

Unconventional Warfare Operations: "Operations which are conducted within enemy or enemy-controlled territory by predominantly indigenous personnel, usually supported and directed in varying degrees by an external source."

1
BATTLEFIELD LOG:
The Congo—July, 1960

The Belgian Congo, renamed the Republic of Zaire in 1971, is about one-fourth the size of the United States. Geographers and topographers would say that its central region is a vast, low-lying plateau consisting mostly of tropical rain forest, with terraced mountains to the east and west, savanna in the south and southeast, and grasslands to the north. But any soldier who has fought there will say that it's all jungle and jungle shrub, with a few grassy clearings, an occasional hill, and numerous rivers and streams—most of which run into one of the largest, muddiest, snake- and crocodile-infested rivers in the world: the Congo River (now the Zaire River).

The earliest inhabitants of this sprawling land appear to have been the Pygmies, who are still to be found hidden away in the savanna areas and the less-populated regions. The country was later inhabited by the Bantu tribes who migrated from the eastern nations of Tanzania, Ruanda-Urundi, and Uganda. In the fifteenth century, Portuguese explorers visited the land and discovered that most of the Congo and Angola were ruled by the powerful Bantu Bakongo kingdom, but there appears also to have been some influence from a migration of the Nilotic tribes from Sudan in the north. Eighty percent of the inhabitants of the Congo are still members or descendants of the Bantu tribes, with the remainder of the populace belonging to some two hundred smaller tribes and ethnic groups. French is the official language, but various Bantu dialects are more prolific—particularly outside the major cities and in the nation's vast hinterland.

In 1878 the British explorer Henry Stanley, who had spent almost all of 1877 exploring the Congo, was retained by King Leopold II of Belgium. He was sent back to the Congo to persuade the native chiefs that they would be better off under the protection of the king of Belgium. The Bantus, knowing no better, were reasonably receptive to the idea, and at the Conference of Berlin in 1884–1885, the Congo Free State was organized with King Leopold II as owner and ruler.

Unrest in the country during the years 1901 to 1907, as a result of gross exploitation of native labor in the rubber plantations, brought severe international criticism, and in 1908 the Congo was changed from a free state to a colony of Belgium.

By January 1960, civil unrest, insurgency, guerrilla war, and world opinion—inspired mostly by Soviet and Chinese Communists—forced Belgium into giving the Congo its independence. June 30, 1960, was set as Independence Day, and in the preceding six months various groups from all regions of the nation used subversion and force to establish the right to govern. Groups of armed raiders indiscriminately attacked towns and villages, killing natives and white foreigners alike, but the Belgian Army managed to maintain reasonable control until Independence Day.

All Asians, white Americans, and white Europeans had been advised by their governments and the

Belgian government to leave the country before June 30, as their safety could not be guaranteed when the country received its independence. Assurances came from the newly elected premier of the Congolese national government, Patrice Lumumba, that all whites and Asians would be safe. The Belgian government, however, requested that such assurances be ignored; their intelligence sources indicated that a massive antiforeigner campaign, nurtured by years of suppressed jealousy and hate, would be launched by rivals of Premier Lumumba. The Belgian government was also aware of the fact that certain elements of the Congolese National Army would take part in the bloodletting, and that the remaining national forces who were loyal to Lumumba could not possibly protect all the foreigners.

Thousands of whites and Asians—mostly missionaries, plantation owners, and merchants—maintained an arrogantly naïve belief that they knew better than the Belgian security forces, and they chose to stay.

Prior to July 1, the Belgian government started to withdraw the majority of its troops, and the violence level increased, with most of the attacks being against foreign missionary outposts and small-plantation owners. On July 1, a wave of violence, directed mostly against white men, women, and children, swept across the nation. Reports flooded into the capital city, Leopoldville (now Kinshasa), with stories of half-crazed rebel troops burning and looting missions, plantations, and small towns and villages. The reports also showed that such raids were accompanied by killings, beatings, torture, rape of nuns and foreign women.

As predicted, units of the Congolese National Army revolted and joined the other rebel groups in a spree of atrocities. The remaining Belgian troops were hard pressed to respond to all the calls for help.

The United States Ambassador, Clare Timberlake, immediately set to work to try to rescue American and

European residents in the outlying areas. Timberlake's plea to Washington for specialized military assistance was considered carefully, since a massive force of American troops could not be sent to the Congo without an invitation from the national government. Premier Lumumba refused to invite American troops to restore order, insisting that the whites who had remained were not really being threatened, and that his own forces, with help from the remaining Belgian paratroopers, would eventually bring the "small band of troublemakers" to justice.

Lumumba, it appears, was living in the same dream world as that in which the foreigners had lived before the country's independence. But the United States was not living in a dream world. In response to Ambassador Timberlake's request and to advice from the Belgian government, the Pentagon was ordered by President Dwight D. Eisenhower to assist the State Department by sending a small, highly trained group of unconventional-warfare specialists to assist the Belgian paratroopers in the rescue of American citizens. The group was to be under the direct control of the State Department—namely, Ambassador Timberlake—and they were not to wear or display United States military uniforms.

Prior to June 30, 1960, Colonel (later to become Brigadier General) "Iron Mike" Paulick, Commanding Officer, 10th Special Forces Group, Bad Tolz, Germany, had been carefully following events in the Congo. As the violence and atrocities increased toward the end of June, and as a considerable amount of it was directed against the American white population, Paulick suspected that a request might be received for Special Forces assistance. He kept these thoughts to himself until after Congolese Independence Day.

When the violence increased dramatically, Paulick

decided that it might be worthwhile to make some preparations. He sent for Lieutenant Sully Fontaine, a highly intelligent and experienced warrior in the field of unconventional warfare.

Sully Fontaine, having been born in Belgium, spoke French better than he spoke English. Before joining the United States Army, he had been a British Special Operations Executive agent during World War II, and had been parachuted into France to fight behind the German lines. He also worked with the British Special Air Service Regiment and the American Office of Strategic Services in the later stages of the war. He had been commissioned in the Belgian Army and had seen extensive service with one of the famous Belgian parachute regiments in the Congo. Further, he had a knowledge of the main Bantu dialect, and he had an avid personal interest in African affairs, with a particular interest in the Congo.

Iron Mike Paulick knew that Fontaine was a highly capable leader of men and an extremely fast thinker in emergency situations. He ordered Fontaine to select a small team and to prepare it for a hasty departure from Bad Tolz. When the names of the six-man team were presented to Paulick, he realized that Fontaine was preparing for almost any eventuality.

All the individuals Sully Fontaine had chosen spoke French fluently. For his second-in-command he had selected Captain Jake Clements, who was known as "The Snake" because of his incredible skill and expertise in jungle warfare and survival. The fact that a second-in-command outranked a team leader was, and still is, of no consequence in most Special Forces operations. The Snake wanted to be part of the team in any capacity, and he would not have complained even if Fontaine—who knew the area of operation and had the necessary leadership abilities—had been a private.

The remaining members of the team were Master

Sergeant Steve Sobiachevsky, Russian-born and fluent in his native language as well as French; Master Sergeant George Yosich, who had led teams of guerrilla fighters behind the enemy lines in Korea; Master Sergeant "Pop" Grant, a former Navy Underwater Demolition Team member; Master Sergeant Charles Hoskins, a multinational weapons specialist; and, finally, Master Sergeant Stefan Mazak, Czechoslovakian-born, a former French Foreign Legionnaire and an experienced guerrilla fighter against both Soviet and Nazi forces during World War II.

A few days after Colonel Paulick approved Lieutenant Fontaine's team, his foresight was rewarded. Orders came from Heidelberg, Germany, United States Army Headquarters in Europe, to provide one French-speaking officer with jungle-warfare experience for a joint-forces team that was to be placed at Ambassador Timberlake's disposal. Paulick was disappointed, but he managed to negotiate with Army Headquarters and convinced the mission organizers, by reading to them the credentials of some of the men Fontaine had chosen, that they needed at least three Special Forces team members.

Fontaine chose Captain Jake (The Snake) Clements and Master Sergeant Stefan Mazak to make up his small Special Forces detachment, and they left Bad Tolz and traveled to the United States Air Force base at Rhine Main, Germany, to join the rest of the rescue team.

On their arrival at Rhine Main they met the other members of the team: two Army officers and one Air Force shortwave-radio expert. Fontaine discovered that they would be provided with several small rescue aircraft when they reached the Congo.

Shortly after their arrival at the Air Force base, they boarded the large transport aircraft that was to take them to Africa.

                    *   *   *

After many long hours of flying, some of them in extremely bad weather, and several refueling stops, they arrived over the Congo.

As their aircraft approached the designated airfield, Fontaine requested the use of a radio headset so that he could listen to the French-speaking air traffic controller. As they touched down on the runway, Fontaine suddenly realized that something was wrong. The air traffic controller seemed very confused as to which aircraft was which. Within a split second, Sully Fontaine realized that they had landed at the wrong airfield. He shouted at the pilot to get airborne again, and the pilot immediately applied full power. When the aircraft lifted into the air, it was followed by a hail of wild and erratic gunfire from ground installations.

Although the aircraft was hit by rifle fire, no serious damage was done and the lumbering craft managed to get clear of the area without further trouble. When they were safely away from the rather unfriendly airfield, the confusion was cleared up and the correct airfield was located. Despite repeated assurances from the air traffic controller that it was quite safe to land, the pilot insisted on circling the airfield several times to have a good look before he attempted to land.

Ambassador Timberlake explained to Lieutenant Fontaine that all evacuation and rescue missions at major airfields would be carried out by the Belgian paratroopers and the Belgian Air Force. All other operations—those into smaller, less secure airfields, rough landing strips, and jungle clearings—would be taken care of by the Special Forces team and their light aircraft.

Five days after Fontaine and his men landed in the Congo, a mixed fleet of six rescue aircraft arrived. Three were conventional fixed-wing aircraft and three were helicopters. The fixed-wing craft were all single-engine—two fourteen-passenger de Havilland Otters, and one seven-passenger de Havilland Beaver—and were noted for their ability to operate from short, rough airfields and jungle clearings. The helicopters were the large, twin-rotor, United States Navy Piasecki H-21 craft, which were capable of carrying fourteen passengers and were commonly referred to as "Flying Bananas" because of their peculiar shape. The pilots of all the aircraft were volunteers who had been carefully selected for their flying skills, bush-flying experience, and knowledge of the French language.

The base of operations for the rescue mission was established at the airfield of Coquilhatville (now Mbandaka), which was securely held by the Belgian paratroopers. With the arrival of their own aircraft, which were completely unarmed, the Special Forces group went to work to establish their operation.

Most of the missionary outposts used shortwave radios to communicate with the major cities in the Congo, and it was their principal means of calling for help. The Air Force radio specialist, who had brought with him some of the most modern shortwave radio communications available, played a vital part in the operation, since his specialized equipment could pick up calls for help from even the weakest of transmitters.

Once established in Coquilhatville, the team began to respond to calls for assistance from the isolated groups. They flew to remote airfields, jungle clearings, river sandbars, and almost any area large enough for their aircraft to operate from. Where the fixed-wing craft could not land, the helicopters could—and when even the helicopters could not land, ropes were lowered to the people on the ground.

For normal rescue operations, Fontaine organized a system for the aircraft to work in pairs. In response to a call for help, the two aircraft would fly to the designated landing area, where only one of the craft would land while the other circled overhead. The aircraft that landed would taxi reasonably close to the waiting group of refugees, but the pilot would be prepared to take off immediately if it was an ambush or if anything went wrong. One member of Fontaine's team, dressed in civilian clothes and armed only with concealed hand grenades, would approach the group of refugees. As he did this, he would be covered by a man with a submachine gun from the back of the waiting aircraft until it had been established that the waiting group were genuine refugees. If things were not quite right, the man approaching the refugees would give a hand signal, and the submachine gun would immediately open fire to cover his retreat to the aircraft. Once it was established that the group were indeed refugees, the second aircraft would be signaled to land and everyone would be quickly flown out.

This system worked very well. During their first nine days of operation the team rescued almost 240 missionaries of various denominations without suffering a single casualty. There were several minor incidents in which the aircraft picked up a few bullet holes, but no serious damage was done.

On one occasion, a desperate call for help came from a priest in the Gwendje area, a considerable distance east of Coquilhatville, which caused a departure from the normal procedure. The priest's radio message was very weak, but he made it clear that his request was urgent—his missionary outpost was under attack by a large group of rebels. As only one aircraft was immediately available, Sully Fontaine and Stefan Mazak took off in it and flew toward Gwendje in an attempt to locate the mission and determine how many people needed to be rescued. They left instructions that as soon as one of the other aircraft returned to

Coquilhatville it was to be prepared to fly out to assist
them.

When they landed at the airstrip near Gwendje,
they found no refugees and there seemed to be no sign
of trouble in the immediate area. Fontaine had managed to tell the priest to fly a flag from the roof of the
building they were in, but Fontaine saw no flag and
nothing in the area that resembled a missionary building. He instructed Mazak to remain at the airstrip while
he and the pilot took off to search the area from the air.

Stefan Mazak was a sharp-eyed and intelligent
warrior. He was short, stocky, and possessed incredible
physical strength. When Fontaine left him he was
carrying a radio, grenades, and a submachine gun, and
more ammunition than two average Special Forces soldiers could carry between them. Without question,
Mazak was an ideal warrior, both for his quick thinking
and his physical attributes.

Fontaine and the pilot located a small village about
ten miles to the east. On top of one of the buildings was
a small flag. There was no airstrip or suitable clearing,
but the pilot skillfully landed on one of the dirt roads
that led straight to the village. He brought the aircraft
to a halt about one hundred yards from the building
with the flag on top, and Fontaine quickly climbed out
and ordered the pilot to take off and hold overhead.

As the aircraft lifted into the air, Fontaine, wearing
a British safari jacket, shorts, boots, and a bush hat,
started walking toward the building with the flag. He
was carrying a portable radio and, apart from two
concealed grenades, was unarmed. As he approached
the building he saw a priest emerge and heard faint
sounds of rifle and machine-gun fire a short distance
away.

The priest confirmed that it was he who had called
for help. He then led Fontaine into the building, where

there were twelve people who had to be evacuated. Six of them were nuns who had been raped repeatedly, tortured, and beaten, and were in desperate need of medical treatment. The priest informed Fontaine that they had made several attempts to get away from the village, but on each occasion they had been discovered by the soldiers, who the priest estimated were about fifty to a hundred in number, and further atrocities had been perpetrated on the nuns.

The soldiers could still be heard at the other end of the village, engaged in a wild spree of raiding and looting. They had promised the priest that they would be back to kill all of them. Fontaine, realizing that he had little time to spare, contacted Sergeant Mazak on the portable radio. The reception was very poor, but Fontaine managed to make it clear to Mazak that he needed a platoon of Belgian soldiers to assist and an additional aircraft to get the refugees out. The sergeant promised to do his best.

Fontaine organized his small party and moved them out of the building and down the road to where the aircraft would land. Just as they reached the spot, a great yelling horde of at least a hundred rebel soldiers came charging toward them from the village. The wild-eyed and ragged rebels were armed with rifles, pistols, and machine guns, which they fired repeatedly into the air and into the jungle at apparently invisible targets.

As the rebels approached, the terrified refugees crowded together behind Fontaine, who watched the frenzied mob carefully and singled out a big, mean-looking man who appeared to be the leader. The man, insisting that he be addressed as a major, announced to the refugees that they were all going to die. Fontaine calmly asked him if he would step aside for a quiet word. The man laughed loudly and agreed, but informed Fontaine that it would make no difference, since he had instructions to kill all whites.

As they stepped aside, Fontaine quickly produced a grenade, pulled out the pin, and gave it to the self-titled major. The major held the pin and stared in horror at the grenade in Fontaine's hand. Fontaine informed him that if anyone fired a shot at the refugees or at himself, the major would most certainly die with them.

The terrified major tried to move away, but Fontaine moved with him and slowly started to release his grip on the grenade in front of the man's face. The major, his eyes bulging, screamed at his mob to stop moving and stop shooting. They obeyed their frightened leader and silently watched his trousers darken as he lost control of his bladder.

For the next two hours an incredible scene took place. The major continually begged his men not to shoot at anything or anyone; and every time he moved, Sully Fontaine moved with him. The pressure of a grenade firing lever is not very great, but after two hours, despite the fact that Fontaine was carefully shifting it from one hand to the other, it began to feel like a ton. He was beginning to worry that his ruse would fail, for the rebels were getting very restless and were considering shooting both their leader and the refugees.

The additional rescue aircraft had arrived overhead and were circling steadily. They would not land until they received the signal from Fontaine, but he could not give it since Mazak and the Belgian paratroopers had not yet arrived.

When Stefan Mazak received Sully Fontaine's message, he immediately contacted the Belgians at Coquilhatville, who told him they would parachute the soldiers in to help Fontaine. Mazak told them to forget the air drop—the paratroopers would be too vulnerable—and just to send them in one of the de Havilland

Otters, and to pick him up on their way through. When they replied that they would have to think about that, Mazak contacted his own radio operator and ordered him to get one of the de Havilland Otters on its way to Gwendje to pick him up.

On learning that it would be about an hour before the aircraft arrived, Mazak gave instructions to forget about him and to send the Otter straight to the area where Fontaine was. He then tightened all the straps on his ammunition packs and radio, to prevent them from bouncing against his body, and started out at a fast pace through the jungle toward Fontaine and the refugees. As he fought his way through shrub and brush, Stefan Mazak was unaware of the drama that was taking place between Fontaine and the rebels. His instincts, however, told him that all was not well, and he did not slacken his pace, nor did he dump any of his ammunition or equipment to lighten his load during the ten-mile run.

As he approached the village he saw the two aircraft circling overhead and became more cautious. When he spotted the group of rebels and the tiny band of refugees, he maneuvered himself so that he could come straight out of the undergrowth close to Fontaine.

By this time the rebels were agitated and were starting to move around, and Sully Fontaine was almost certain that his ploy was going to fail. To add to his problems, his hands were aching from holding the firing lever on the grenade for almost two hours. Just when he began to think that everything was lost, he heard a rustle in the undergrowth. The slight noise turned into a tremendous crashing sound as Mazak suddenly burst from the undergrowth.

Mazak was an awesome sight with his face and arms bathed in sweat mixed with dirt and green slime from the jungle foliage. He was screaming and yelling in the most foul Legionnaire French imaginable, and he started firing his submachine gun in every direction.

Fontaine almost burst out laughing as he threw the grenade in among the rebels. The explosion, followed by Mazak's fire bearing directly onto them, caused the rebels to flee in disarray.

Fontaine signaled the rescue aircraft to land, while Mazak, still screaming torrents of abuse in Legionnaire French, chased the soldiers into the jungle. As the last of the refugees were being loaded into the aircraft, Mazak returned to the road and apologized to Fontaine for the delay. He explained that he had tried desperately to hurry the Belgian paratroopers, but that they had been too slow for him so he had finally decided to race to the village by himself. Fontaine smiled, thanked him, and acknowledged that Stefan Mazak, who was supposed to be ten miles away, was the last person he had expected to see coming out of the undergrowth to save his life.

After almost a month of rescue missions, the turmoil seemed to settle down and the entire Special Forces team, with the exception of Lieutenant Sully Fontaine, left the Congo.

At the request of Ambassador Clare Timberlake, Sully Fontaine remained in the Congo for another two months, and proved to be of invaluable assistance to both the ambassador and his staff during several other somewhat delicate diplomatic situations.

Stefan Mazak returned to Bad Tolz. He was later to distinguish himself in Vietnam, where he finally gave his life for his adopted country. If Stefan Mazak's actions in the Congo had occurred during "open conflict" between the United States and another nation, they would have earned him a decoration for his courage and skill. However, at the time of the action, the world political situation was such that any word of the presence of a handful of United States Army Special Forces soldiers involved in daring rescue missions in the Congo would have been very unwise.

Ambassador Timberlake, in his confidential reports to the State Department, did recommend that the highest praise be afforded to Lieutenant Sully Fontaine, Master Sergeant Stefan Mazak, Captain Jake Clements, and the entire rescue team. Without them, a considerable number of United States citizens, and citizens of several other friendly nations, would certainly have perished.

2
HISTORICAL DEVELOPMENT OF THE SPECIAL FORCES

According to the United States Army, today's Special Forces are the direct descendants of the combined American and Canadian First Special Service Force, otherwise known as the "Devil's Brigade," which fought in Europe during the World War II. However, apart from the words *Special* and *Force*, and the unquestionable bravery and fighting ability of the World War II group, there is no other reasonable comparison that can be made with today's Special Forces.

The First Special Service Force was a large, highly trained conventional unit—more of a Ranger-style brigade than anything else—whereas the present-day Special Forces were formed for one specific reason: to teach and fight guerrilla and counterguerrilla warfare.

The true ancestor, or predecessor, of the Special Forces is the Office of Strategic Services, usually referred to as the OSS.

The OSS was organized and led by the brilliant Major General William J. "Wild Bill" Donovan in 1942. When he first proposed that America should have a military organization that specialized in guerrilla warfare operations—similar to the British Special Operations Executive—Donovan knew that the Chiefs of Staff for the Army and the Navy would be somewhat opposed to the idea. But he was greatly surprised at the intensity of their opposition. He was even more surprised when the Federal Bureau of Investigation joined the opposition—until he discovered that they had been planning to form an international intelligence organization and intended that it come under their direct control (the Central Intelligence Agency did not exist at that time).

However, despite the opposition from the Army and the Navy, Donovan was convinced that any such organization should be a military one, since he believed that it was vital for the success of the war in Europe and the Pacific, and he persisted in his attempts to recruit support for the idea. When it became obvious to him that the Chiefs of Staff and the leaders of every official intelligence organization in the nation were completely against his idea, he went directly to President Franklin D. Roosevelt. The two men had a longstanding personal relationship, and when Donovan explained his ideas the President immediately issued orders for the formation of the OSS, much to the disdain of the opposition.

Wild Bill Donovan traveled to England to meet "Intrepid," the code name given to the head of the British Special Operations Executive (SOE), to seek assistance in forming the OSS. At that time, the SOE had almost two years' experience in placing agents behind the German lines in France, Holland, Belgium, and other occupied nations. Apart from gathering intelligence information, the main task of these agents was to organize and train members of the European resistance movements in guerrilla warfare.

The SOE willingly gave Donovan all the assistance necessary, including the training of OSS personnel, but they refused to participate in joint operations because

Intrepid felt it was far too risky to put inexperienced agents in the field. However, just as Donovan and President Roosevelt were friends, Intrepid and Prime Minister Winston Churchill were friends, and it appears that a meeting was held between the four men, where Churchill persuaded Intrepid to engage in joint operations with the OSS.

The combined operations in Europe were highly successful, and so, too, were almost all the individual operations that the OSS became involved with after their initial cooperative efforts with the British.

In the Pacific theater, General Douglas A. MacArthur would not permit the OSS to operate as a unit. He had vehemently opposed the formation of the OSS and insisted that he had no use for them in his sphere of operations. Although Donovan tried to persuade Roosevelt to influence the situation, the President decided to respect MacArthur's wishes.

However, apart from operations in Europe, the OSS was also highly successful in other areas; of particular note is the success of OSS Detachment 101 in the Burma jungles.

Captain Ray Peers, a brilliant military leader who was later to become one of the few Special Forces proponents to rise to the rank of lieutenant general, led a group of some twenty-five OSS men in training the fierce-fighting, happy, diminutive Kachin tribesmen of northern Burma to engage in guerrilla warfare against the Japanese.

By the end of the war this group of OSS-trained and -organized tribesmen numbered almost 11,000 and had claimed the lives of nearly 10,000 Japanese soldiers, with a loss of only 206 of their own.

General Joseph ("Vinegar Joe") Stilwell, commander of the Burma theater and known for his sour disposition and skepticism, once confronted Peers and the native leader of a small, successful Kachin guerrilla group.

Peers and the Kachin leader had submitted an after-action report showing the number of enemy killed. Stilwell felt the number was too high and dourly demanded to know how they could be so inaccurate. Before Peers could reply, the tiny Kachin guerrilla leader produced a bamboo tube, emptied its contents on the table, and said in broken English, "Please Sir General, you divide by two." Stilwell stared in horror at the pile of dried, wrinkled human ears that lay in front of him before he stormed away—never again to question a Kachin kill tally. Ray Peers is reported to have said that it took him almost six months to stop the Kachins from cutting the ears off those they had killed, but he was never certain that this practice stopped completely.

Apart from the high attrition rate of enemy soldiers, the Burma theater commanders credited more than 90 percent of their intelligence information on the Japanese Army to the OSS and their Kachin Rangers. The United States Tenth Air Force, known as the "Burma Bridge Busters," claimed that more than 80 percent of their targets were located and designated by the same group.

When President Roosevelt died, so did the Office of Strategic Services. Although the OSS had been in existence only three years, it had performed exactly as Donovan had stated it would. It had been a resounding success, but that did not matter to the hierarchy of the Army, Navy, and FBI, who had been seeking every opportunity to discredit the OSS and to have it disbanded. Without Roosevelt, Donovan lost the battle to keep the organization alive, and President Harry S. Truman ordered that it be disbanded in 1945. When this occurred, most of the members of the OSS left the military at the end of the war feeling that they were not quite suited to life in a peacetime army.

A small number of the veteran members of the OSS did continue with their military service and joined the Central Intelligence Group of the National Intelligence Agency. (The CIG officially became the CIA with the passage of the National Security Act on September 18, 1947, and it is interesting to note that the present-day CIA considers the OSS to be its birthplace and, consequently, Donovan to be its founding father.)

One advocate of the value of guerrilla warfare who remained with the Army was Colonel Russell Volkmann. He had been the leader of the Filipino guerrillas on the island of Luzon during World War II, and when he returned to the United States he was sent to Fort Benning, Georgia.

Colonel Volkmann set to work producing two field manuals on guerrilla warfare. At the same time, he and several others were constantly trying to persuade their leaders in Washington that there was a need for a special force.

Their unconventional theories and ideas fell on deaf ears and closed minds during the late 1940s, despite the fact that events in Europe were not going well for the free world, particularly when Joseph Stalin demonstrated his intentions by sealing off the city of Berlin. Stalin's Red Army surrounded Berlin in April 1948, and revealed, to the astonishment of the remainder of the free world, that the Union of Soviet Socialist Republics had not demobilized at the end of World War II; it had virtually remobilized. It was now much better equipped than it had ever been and was well advanced in the development of a nuclear capacity. The balance of nonnuclear military power in the world obviously lay in the hands of the Soviets, and by 1949 almost everyone in Europe, including the member nations of the newly formed North Atlantic Treaty Organization (NATO), believed that World War III was close at hand.

Intelligence sources of the day suggested that the Soviets would attempt to take the remainder of Europe by force within four or five years; it was obvious that they had the military strength to do so without much effort. The use of nuclear weapons to stop them was considered, but was ruled out because nuclear retaliatory action by the Soviets was sure to follow, and that would certainly cause the destruction of Europe. The situation was simply a standoff, and has remained that way ever since.

However, during 1949 and 1950, the threat of Soviet forces invading Europe finally caused some of the closed minds in the Pentagon to open, and it was decided that preparations should be made to establish some basis for a resistance movement in the event that an invasion did take place.

In June 1950, the military planners were still pondering the matter when the Korean War began. It was obvious that nuclear weapons could not be used to push back the North Koreans—world opinion would not support their use. The conventional war that followed in Korea was not just a repeat of World War II; it was almost a repeat of the trench warfare of World War I, much to the confusion of the military strategists.

As Commander in Chief, General MacArthur saw his Eighth Army being harried from behind their own lines by North Korean guerrillas. He was highly annoyed at this and demanded that his forces engage in similar tactics behind the North Korean front lines. But the capability did not exist, as the Pentagon planners had already discovered in their attempts to establish a network for future resistance movements in Europe. What was desperately needed was the OSS, but it did not exist, and the CIA did not have the means or the experience to set up and train guerrilla fighters.

MacArthur's demands resulted in a sudden interruption in Russell Volkmann's literary life at Fort Benning when he was ordered to present himself immediately at MacArthur's headquarters in Tokyo, Japan.

On his arrival he was told simply that he was to take command of all operations behind enemy lines, but he quickly discovered that no operational units existed and that he was expected to establish, organize, and train such units—starting with nothing more than himself.

It was immediately obvious to Volkmann that neither MacArthur nor his staff had even the slightest idea of what was required to train personnel and establish a support system for behind-the-lines or unconventional warfare operations. Despite his protests that it would take a considerable amount of time to produce the size and type of operational unit that MacArthur wanted, Volkmann was ordered to produce results almost immediately.

Although he knew that everything was against his getting the kind of organization that was required, he became totally involved in planning and organizing, and he slowly started to gather some key personnel. Unfortunately, the long, hard hours of work and the constant battling with the stereotypical military attitude of MacArthur's staff took its toll. Volkmann became ill and had to be evacuated to the States just as the planning and basic organizational parts of the task were completed.

What followed when he left was both confusing and relatively unsuccessful.

Various units were formed, and they did see action behind the North Korean lines, but it appears that they were landed by boat and the missions were of short duration. The missions were in effect commando raids; without distracting from the sincerity and courage of the men who performed them, the operations could not be classed as guerrilla warfare. No reports or after-action records are available to show any real measure of success, and, sadly, most of the veterans who were involved in the operations seem to feel that their efforts achieved little or nothing.

The Korean ceasefire peace talks began in July 1951, and the fighting eventually stopped on July 27, 1953. However, by early 1952, the lack of success of the hastily formed special operations units finally convinced some of our senior military leaders that a different approach was required.

Most significantly, they realized that in order to conduct successful unconventional warfare operations, preparations such as planning, selection of personnel and specialized equipment, establishment of support organizations, and training of all concerned were required well in advance of the start of any war or conflict.

One of the Pentagon's supporters of unconventional warfare was General Robert McClure. He had under his control a Psychological Operations Staff Unit, within which was hidden a Special Warfare Division. McClure had quietly recruited some of the best unconventional-warfare specialists in the Army, including Volkmann, who had recovered from his illness on his return from Korea. Others in the group were Colonel Aaron Bank, former OSS; Colonel Wendell Fertig, former leader of the Filipino guerrillas; Colonel Joe Waters, former OSS and Merrill's Marauders; Colonel Robert McDowell, former OSS; and several other experienced guerrilla and unconventional-warfare specialists of the European, Balkan, and Indochina theaters during World War II.

McClure and his Special Warfare Division started to campaign among the Army Chiefs at the Pentagon for the establishment of a large, permanent special-forces organization in Europe in preparation for the start of

World War III. They met with incredible resistance, despite the fact that the Army Chief of Staff, General J. Lawton Collins, supported the idea.

After considerable argument, McClure's group succeeded in obtaining approval for a total peacetime force of twenty-five hundred personnel. However, they soon discovered that, although the battle with their opponents among the Army hierarchy was tough, there was an even tougher battle to be fought with the combined forces of the State Department, the CIA, and the Air Force.

Unknown to almost everyone in government and military circles—including the Joint Chiefs of Staff—the two most recently formed services, the Air Force and the CIA, with encouragement from the State Department, had been secretly developing plans to form an unconventional-warfare organization that would completely exclude the other services.

The Air Force/CIA/State Department concept was that the Air Force would have a massive air-strike capability and would use it to pound the enemy into disarray, at which point the CIA guerrillas, parachuted in from Air Force craft, would move in to finish off the job on the ground. As ludicrous as it may sound, it was their belief that the Army, Navy, and Marine Corps should simply be reduced, both in size and in structure, and confined to a policing role.

The reason for the involvement and support given by the State Department was unclear, but it appears that some of its senior members were still upset at the Army Chiefs of Staff who had prevented them from having an active role during World War II. Another factor was their obvious displeasure at the President's appointment of military personnel to lucrative consular positions overseas at the end of the war (such positions were normally appointed and filled by members of the State Department).

When the Air Force/CIA/State Department group heard of the Army's intentions they immediately objected, and presented their own plan. What ensued can only be described as a bitter interservice governmental brawl, and it seems that General McClure resorted to the use of a friendship to get President Truman to intervene.

The result was that the Army received the guerrilla-warfare and special-forces mission, while the Air Force was charged with establishing some small Air Resupply and Communications Wings to support them. However, the Army interdepartmental and the general interservice rivalry and resentment that had built up during the squabble was to cause considerable heel-dragging and lack of cooperation during the formative years of the Special Forces.

The first display of ill feeling came in April 1952, when Colonel Aaron Bank was sent to Fort Bragg, North Carolina, to establish the Special Forces Group. He was instructed to report to the small, recently established Psychological Warfare Center, located in a remote area of the Fort Bragg complex, and ordered to set up the Special Forces operation. Despite Colonel Bank's and Colonel Volkmann's objections to the Special Forces being deliberately hidden under the Psychological Warfare umbrella, the Pentagon was adamant. Special Forces, the Army hierarchy felt, was in the same "foul play" arena as Psy War, and that was where it would be based.

Colonel Bank recruited a handful of suitable men to help him form the basis of a unit, and on June 20, 1952, with a total complement of ten men, the 10th Special Forces Group (Airborne) was formed.

Bank had found some willing former OSS and Ranger battalion men, as well as a few serious-minded Airborne soldiers, who were looking for something different. From that point his men did their own recruiting by word of mouth. As the unit grew, Bank realized that almost all of his men were professional Airborne non-commissioned officers.

They were thoroughly dedicated soldiers who quietly recruited further select personnel from among their peer group. However, as the unit grew, they knew that they needed a cadre of commissioned officers in order to meet Army requirements; otherwise they would automatically be the recipients of some undesirable "volunteer" second lieutenants straight out of West Point. Consequently, the noncommissioned officers sought out a few commissioned officers who they felt were the right material. Once established in the Special Forces Group, the commissioned officers then sought out friends who they felt were suited to the job; the result was the building of a superbly qualified officer cadre, without one dreaded rookie second lieutenant.

This somewhat unorthodox method of selecting officers satisfied Aaron Bank, who was acutely aware of the fact that very few good career-minded officers would entertain the idea of joining the Special Forces—it would be a definite mark against them by the more conventional-minded military leaders when promotions were being allocated.

The training program at Fort Bragg was intensive, both physically and mentally, and the Group participated in major military exercises throughout the United States, acting as infiltrators and saboteurs and generally functioning in the role of guerrillas. They caused a considerable amount of disruption in some nicely planned war games and became very unpopular with most field commanders. On several occasions an entire exercise was called to a halt before it was completed and the Special Forces men were asked to remove themselves because of their "dirty tricks."

By the time the 10th Special Forces Group was

one year old, it had a complement of a little more than seven hundred men. It was a remarkable collection of physically fit, disciplined, highly cross-trained, multilingual, professional soldiers. A considerable number were foreign-born—there were Dutchmen, Belgians, Poles, Hungarians, Danes, Finns, Czechs, and a few Russians—and had extensive resistance, guerrilla, and unconventional-warfare fighting experience from World War II. Many had served in the OSS, the British SOE and SAS, the German Army, the French Foreign Legion, and the French Maquis.

Most of these men had joined the American Army under the legislation known as the Lodge Bill, which permitted foreigners to achieve American citizenship by serving with the American Armed Forces. Those who gravitated to the 10th Special Forces did so because they were born warriors and had a particular liking for unconventional warfare. Aaron Bank and his senior staff members selected these men because of their attitude, fighting experience, native language, and teaching skills. There was a particular emphasis on teaching skills, as a prerequisite of all Special Forces, both then and now, is the ability to instruct others.

In June 1953, a workers' revolt in Soviet-occupied East Berlin was savagely quelled by the Red Army. This somewhat small incident alarmed the Joint Chiefs of Staff, who realized that if further revolts occurred in Eastern Europe, the Special Forces at Fort Bragg were definitely in the wrong place. As a result, they decided to move the entire 10th Special Forces Group to a new headquarters in southern Germany, near the town of Bad Tolz in the Bavarian Alps.

They had no sooner announced their intentions than the CIA, which had no operating jurisdiction (and never had) within the United States, in conjunction with the State Department made a final attempt to

break up and confine the deployment of Special Forces
to purely wartime situations. They spread the rumor
that the 10th Special Forces was ragged, amateurish,
undisciplined, and totally unprepared and unfit for
deployment in Europe.

The Joint Chiefs of Staff were forced to send an
experienced investigator to Fort Bragg to make an
independent assessment. Ray Peers, the leader of the
OSS Burma Operations and now a full colonel, was
approved by all concerned parties to be the impartial
investigator, and he was dispatched to Fort Bragg.

Peers quickly discovered that everything in the
Special Forces seemed to come in threes. All the men
were triple volunteers—Army, Airborne, and Special
Forces; almost all had three stripes (sergeants') and
were fully qualified in at least three Military Occupational Specialties; most had a knowledge of three lan-
guages; and the vast majority of them had been in
combat three times or more. He found no fresh young
faces, no second lieutenants, no privates, no long hair,
and no sloppy or insubordinate attitudes. He did, however, find receptive and adaptable minds—and quite a
few of his own men from the days of the Kachin
Rangers in the Burma jungles.

His report to the Joint Chiefs of Staff is perhaps
one of the most brief on military record: "The men of
the 10th Special Forces Group (Airborne) are ready."

When Colonel Peers departed, half of the existing
10th Special Forces Group prepared for their move to
Europe; the remainder prepared themselves to become
the basis for a new, as yet undesignated, Special Forces
Group.

On a cold day in November 1953, almost the
entire European contingent arrived in Wilmington, North
Carolina, to board a troopship that was bound for the

port of Bremerhaven, at the tip of the Heligoland Bight in the North Sea.

The giant troopship had been loaded in New York with thousands of regular troops destined for service in West Germany. Under normal circumstances it would have sailed straight across the Atlantic, but shortly after putting to sea the ship's captain, on secret orders, diverted to Wilmington to collect "further troops" who had been unable to get to the New York embarkation camps. The captain was suspicious about this unknown group of soldiers because he had been ordered to allocate quarters for them that were as far removed from the other troops as possible.

The Army had made no attempt to send the 10th Special Forces to New York; their existence had been kept as secret as possible even within the Army itself. New York was not the place from which to embark a secret unit, since troopship departures and arrivals at the premier port city in the nation were always grand affairs, accompanied by fanfares from military bands, thousands of tearful families and girl friends, and, worst of all, hordes of story-hungry newspaper correspondents.

For added safety, the 10th were issued new, unmarked jackets and hats for the journey from Fort Bragg to the Wilmington docks. Orders were given that no badges of rank or insignia were permitted to be seen, and the unit's name would not be disclosed to the other troops on board the ship until it was at least three hours out to sea.

As the troopship docked in Wilmington, the rails were lined with curious soldiers and members of the ship's crew. The ship's captain became even more curious as he watched some seven hundred men, dressed like recruits, march onto the pier. The soldiers already on board whistled and jeered and shouted the traditional abuses normally reserved for recruits or green troops.

The Special Forces men had expected it and did

not respond; they simply boarded in silence and were directed to their quarters. Three hours later, they changed into their normal street uniforms and marched on deck, to the amazement of the other troops. Triple chevrons, Airborne patches, and medal ribbons clearly displayed the kind of "raw recruits" they were, and no further abuse was heard.

As the 10th settled in Bad Tolz, the 77th Special Forces Group was formed in Fort Bragg and started to build. Members of the 10th rotated for short duty tours back to Fort Bragg to assist in training and teaching, and qualified members of the 77th were shipped to Bad Tolz for advanced training. By 1956 the two Special Forces Groups were well established, despite the fact that it had been reduced in size by defense-spending cuts initiated by President Eisenhower and Secretary of State John Foster Dulles.

In June 1956, three officers and thirteen noncommissioned officers from the 77th became the 14th Special Forces Operational Detachment and were sent to Hawaii. Shortly after their arrival there they were sent to Thailand to assist in training Thai forces; from there they went to Taiwan and then to Vietnam for the same purpose. Shortly after the formation of the 14th, another small unit, oddly named the 8,231st Army Special Operations Detachment and comprised of five officers and seventeen noncommissioned officers, was formed and sent to Japan.

One year after the formation of the 14th, these two units had been moved to Okinawa to form the basis of the 1st Special Forces Group, since it was believed that the Far East theater needed as much attention as the 10th Special Forces Group was giving the European theater.

By 1960 the three groups were hard at work in their respective areas of operation, with exchanges of personnel between the groups taking place on a regular basis for cross-training purposes.

The total strength of the Army Special Forces at that time was about two thousand men, with the 7th (the redesignated 77th) at Fort Bragg having the largest complement, about nine hundred personnel, the 10th in Bad Tolz with about five hundred, and the 14th in Okinawa with about six hundred.

However, holding that level of manpower was an endless struggle, and the corridors and offices at the Pentagon became the battlefields for the conventional thinkers, who were still trying to get rid of the Special Forces, and the unconventional thinkers, who were simply trying to hold on to what existed.

In 1961, President John F. Kennedy foresaw the threat of wars of liberation through insurgency and guerrilla tactics. He requested our military leaders to prepare for and meet the challenge of the future by increasing our present guerrilla and counterinsurgency forces. To say that everyone jumped on the bandwagon to play to the tune of the new word that President Kennedy had spoken—*counterinsurgency*—would be an understatement. Every department in the government that had any function related to defense or intelligence literally swarmed to the bandwagon. For the armed forces, the direct result was the formation of the SEALs by the Navy, a new and revitalized Air Commando Wing in the Air Force, and an incredible increase in the size of the Army Special Forces.

Shortly after President Kennedy's request was made known, the Army Chiefs of Staff called for an increase in the size of the three Special Forces Groups. They ordered that each group be increased immediately to fifteen hundred personnel and that they expand their operations from guerrilla warfare to counterinsurgency warfare. Included in the same orders were instructions that required preparations to be made for yet further increases in size when the groups reached the fifteen-hundred-personnel level.

The Special Forces leaders, although delighted at the recognition of their value and their increased responsibility, were distressed at the magnitude and complexity of the task. They had been ordered to more than double in size immediately, and it was difficult enough to get quality personnel for their present total complement of two thousand.

As they set to work to formulate plans for rapid growth, President Kennedy visited Fort Bragg and inspected the 7th. He was delighted at what he saw, and when he returned to Washington he said so openly and publicly with the powerful rhetoric for which he was renowned. However, honored though they were, the Special Forces felt they could have done without the publicity, since it resulted in their being inundated with volunteers (from privates to full colonels), requests for interviews from newspaper and television reporters, and further orders from the Pentagon to hurry up and expand.

The Special Warfare Training Center at Fort Bragg turned out about four hundred graduates in 1960. In 1963 it produced more than three thousand, and the veteran Special Forces soldiers began to be embarrassed at the quality of some of the new breed. The rapid growth did cause some lowering of standards, but it also permitted the United States to quickly expand its foreign Military Assistance Program with soldiers who were properly trained for the role. Within a few years, thousands of Special Forces personnel were spread worldwide, training and teaching the armed forces of friendly nations that requested assistance. The Vietnam conflict saw the Special Forces engaged in a classic counterinsurgency and guerrilla battle, which they won. However, the war itself was lost when American forces were withdrawn and the regular troops of the North Vietnamese Army swarmed into South Vietnam.

After Vietnam, the Special Forces were considerably reduced in size, but they continued to train, quietly and without much publicity (more in the manner of the late 1950s than the flamboyant 1960s), but they were again fighting for survival as severe restrictions in defense spending were imposed.

By 1979 the Special Forces were facing further reductions, but the Iranian hostage crisis and various other disturbing situations in friendly Third World nations shocked the Pentagon into a rethink. The Special Forces started to expand again, slowly and steadily, to what they are today—the United States Army's most elite.

3

THE GREEN BERET

The general public and the media normally refer to the United States Army Special Forces as the "Green Berets."

The green beret is, of course, the form of headdress worn by the Army Special Forces. The popular use of the name as a reference to all Special Forces personnel may be attributed to the late President Kennedy, who wrote that the green beret was a symbol of courage and excellence in our armed forces; to the late actor John Wayne, who played the lead role in a motion picture called *The Green Berets;* and to the singer Barry Sadler, who had a hit record of the same name.

Historically, there has probably never been as much squabbling, ill feeling, and fighting over an article of green clothing since 1667, when the Irish Parliament banned the wearing of shamrock and articles of green clothing in public in an attempt to subjugate nationalism among the people of Ireland.

The use of a beret as a form of headdress for elite fighting forces was long ago established in Europe. In the British military, the SAS wore sand-colored berets, the Parachute regiments wore dark red, the Royal

Marine Commando wore dark green, and various other units wore blue or black. In the French military the Foreign Legion Paratroopers also adopted the beret, as did several other nations that had ancestral links with both Britain and France.

Perhaps the first Americans to wear the beret as an official headdress were the members of the joint American/Canadian First Special Service Force (the Devil's Brigade) during World War II. This group wore a bright red beret very similar to that worn by the present-day Combat Control Teams of the Air Force Special Operations Wing (Air Commando). However, the beret was being worn unofficially by some members of the OSS personnel who were on lend-lease assignment with the British SOE.

The wearing of the beret by the Army Special Forces appears to have started in early 1953 as a result of the desire of the men of the newly formed group to be distinct from other Army units. The best documented and substantiated account concerning the origin of the beret with the Special Forces states that it first appeared in a sketch drawn by the now retired Major Herb Brucker (former OSS).

Brucker's original sketch, which showed a Special Forces soldier wearing a camouflage beret, was seen by Lieutenant Roger Pezzelle, who really liked the idea. He submitted an official request for the issue of either camouflage-colored or dark green berets for "the purpose of conducting a field test." However, knowing the Army system, Pezzelle did not wait for officialdom to reply. In the spring of 1953 his own team, Operational Detachment FA 32, was leaving for a lengthy field-training exercise, and Pezzelle purchased enough women's black berets in Fayetteville, North Carolina, for all the members of his detachment.

The original idea was to wear either camouflage or

dark green berets, but Pezzelle could not find any in those colors in North Carolina, so he settled for what he considered the next more conservative color. Although they were women's fashion items—berets were not popular headwear for men in the United States in 1953—the Special Forces soldiers did not mind wearing them, as they doubted that anyone with any sense would poke fun at them.

Pezzelle gave orders to the men in his small detachment that the beret was to be worn only in the field, and he took the precaution of purchasing an extra one that he knew would fit Colonel Aaron Bank, the commanding officer, in the event that the colonel should pay a surprise visit to the field and catch the men wearing an unofficial and unauthorized headdress. Pezzelle's bravery did not stop at the wearing of the beret itself—he also wore his badge of rank on the front of his beret and permitted his men to use their Airborne wings as a cap badge.

At that time, other groups of Special Forces on field exercises or detachment were wearing somewhat more traditional, but not exactly conventional, head gear. Some units wore the woolen "Ernie Pyle" field cap, named after the famous World War II battlefield newspaper correspondent, while others wore either the United States Navy black woolen "watch caps" or Marine Corps field caps. The latter two forms of field headgear, although not authorized, seemed to be a little more accepted by the conventional Army types, perhaps because they actually were issued to other United States military organizations, whereas the beret was "foreign."

The use of unconventional headwear in the field was actually caused by Colonel Bank, as he issued orders that helmets were not to be worn in the field (guerrillas do not wear full military battledress and certainly not helmets). Colonel Bank's orders went so far as to ban helmets for parachute operations, much to the horror of the regimented Airborne jumpmasters in the jump aircraft.

Aaron Bank was accustomed to catching his men in the field wearing Navy watch caps, Marine Corps field caps, and Ernie Pyle caps, but he was quite surprised when he caught Pezzelle's FA 32 wearing the berets. Bank personally liked the berets, but he could not compromise himself by openly condoning such a breach of regulations. What he actually said to Pezzelle is not known; however, it appears that he simply ignored what he saw and quietly warned Pezzelle not to get caught by anyone else.

In November 1953, Pezzelle, now a captain, and Brucker were among those shipped to Bad Tolz with the 10th to establish a base for the Special Forces in Europe. Officialdom still had not replied to Pezzelle's request for a field test of the berets, which did not surprise him or anyone else. But, in fairness to those who had received the request, they had in fact ordered the Army Supply Office to send some berets to Fort Bragg.

The request was an unusual one, since berets were not exactly standard issue, and a search around all the supply offices in the nation began. The method of searching was simple and effective but not speedy. A single document giving the details of what was required was sent out to the nearest supply office. When this office discovered that they did not have any berets, they promptly stamped the document and made a notation that they could not comply with the request. The document was then sent to another depot, which, in turn, did the same when they discovered they had no berets.

As there were no berets in the Army inventory, every supply office in the country received the document, stamped it, made the appropriate notation, and put it back in the system. Eventually the document was returned to the originating supply officer, who, with a clear conscience, decided to spend some of the Army's money. He issued a purchase order for procurement from a civilian source, and when the berets were delivered to the supply officer he immediately sent them on to Fort Bragg.

The procurement took only a year, but when the berets arrived at Fort Bragg, the 77th Special Forces Group was in residence. As no one in the 77th had ordered the berets, and as they had come from an official source, everyone assumed that they were authorized to wear them openly—much to the chagrin of the more conventional military personnel of the Airborne Corps at Fort Bragg. Since there were insufficient berets delivered for the entire 77th, those who were not lucky enough to have them issued promptly went out and ordered them from local stores.

This was not satisfactory, as there was quite a difference between the color and shape of the issued berets and the purchased ones. There was enough opposition to the wearing of the beret from the regular Airborne units as it was, and the various shades of green did not help matters, so the men of the Special Forces decided to do something about it. Surreptitious inquiries quickly revealed that there were no more berets in Army stock and that it would probably take a year to get them through official channels.

In February 1954, the problem was solved when someone unofficially contacted the quartermaster of a Canadian regiment that wore berets. The quartermaster willingly provided the name of the Canadian manufacturer of their berets, the Dorothea Knitting Mills. Once again, unofficial contact was made, and a batch of sample berets was immediately sent to a private address in Fort Bragg. The men of the 77th appropriately chose the color "rifle green," and within twenty-four hours every man in the group had personally paid for at least one beret, although most purchased two.

When the berets arrived, orders were issued by the 77th authorizing the wearing of the beret and prescribing the manner in which it should be worn—although the Army still had not approved it for anything other than a field test. For cap badges, officers were instructed to display their rank, while all others displayed the Airborne wings.

The men of the 10th Special Forces Group were just starting to get themselves organized in Bad Tolz when news reached them that berets had been issued to the 77th in Fort Bragg. Pezzelle and Brucker guessed what had happened—the berets they had ordered for field testing had arrived and someone had wrongfully assumed that it meant they could be worn openly. Pezzelle and Brucker were not disappointed. If the 77th could get away with it amid the spit and polish of the Airborne Corps at Fort Bragg, there was much less chance of trouble in Bad Tolz under the Seventh Army commanders.

With the blessing of their commanding officer, Pezzelle and Brucker set about getting berets for the entire 10th Special Forces Group in Bad Tolz. After extensive inquiries and searching, they discovered that berets, for either men or women, were just not worn by the Germans and there was not a single manufacturer in the nation. Undaunted, Pezzelle and Brucker decided to find someone to make them. They approached a small hatmaking company in Munich, Mutze Muller (*Mutze* means "cap," *Muller* is the family name), which agreed to take on the task.

The German berets were made from three pieces of dark green felt—one large round piece for the top and two pieces for the sides. As a result, the berets were somewhat flatter than the one-piece knitted variety produced by the Canadian Dorothea Mills, but everyone seemed to like them as they were a little more rakish and somewhat daring by comparison to the original "beanie" type.

Pezzelle was not content with officers displaying just their rank and the noncommissioned officers just displaying the Airborne wings, so he set about designing a cap badge, which was to become the unofficial badge of the Special Forces for almost ten years.

Pezzelle had always been amused by the ancient tale of how King Menelaus of Sparta captured the great fortress city of Troy in his efforts to recapture his beautiful wife Helen who had run away with Paris, Prince of Troy. Odysseus the Wily, a great and fabled warrior, is credited with devising the plan to build a large wooden horse that was to be abandoned on the plain of Troy. The horse, of course, was hollow; and inside it were King Menelaus, Odysseus, Diomedes, the great warrior who had battled with and defeated Ares the god of war, Epeus, the builder of the horse, and several other warriors. The Trojans watched the Spartans abandon and burn their camp and then depart from Troy in their ships. All that was left behind was the great wooden horse, which the Trojans proudly dragged into their city as a trophy for their victory. During the night, as the Trojans were celebrating, the ships returned and the Spartan warriors stealthily approached the city walls. The men inside the horse waited until most of the nearby Trojans were asleep before they climbed out of the horse and opened the main gates of the city. The Spartan Army surged into Troy, King Menelaus recaptured his beautiful queen, and the city was destroyed.

It was the deception with the wooden horse that caught Pezzelle's imagination, and he designed a cap badge that depicted the Trojan horse mounted on a shield. In the background, behind the horse, was a bolt of lightning, and at the bottom of the shield were the silver Airborne wings. Pezzelle found a silversmith in Bad Tolz, by the name of Eichmann, who was willing to make a mold and cast the tiny Trojan horses for a reasonable price.

The commanding officer of the 10th Special Forces issued orders authorizing the wearing of the beret with the Trojan-horse badge. However, since neither the beret nor the badge was officially approved by the Army, everyone was warned that should a surprise visit be paid by an unsympathetic Army general, the berets must immediately disappear and be replaced by regulation headwear. A public-address system installed in the barracks in Bad Tolz was used to warn the men whenever such a situation arose, thereby avoiding the possibility of a confrontation.

In general there were few problems concerning the wearing of the beret in Germany, but some serious problems arose in Fort Bragg in 1956. Many veteran Special Forces and 82nd Airborne soldiers who were actively involved in Fort Bragg operations during 1956 are in agreement with the following account of events.

Early in the year there was a large-scale and somewhat prestigious Army field exercise involving not only the Airborne Corps but considerable numbers of other conventional Army units. The men of the 77th Special Forces were elated because, for the first time since their group had been formed, they were being allowed to operate in their unconventional-warfare role during a major exercise within the United States. The fact that it had been decided by the planners that they would be on the "enemy" side, and that they would not win, did not concern the men of the 77th, who simply wanted to show their worth.

The exercise got under way, and within a very short period of time it became obvious that the Army had absolutely no idea what guerrilla warfare was. During the first few days there was enormous confusion. Food, fuel, and ammunition convoys were either ambushed or sent in the opposite direction to which they were supposed to go. Regiments were given false orders over the radio, Airborne troops were dropped safely into the wrong areas, and one general's tactical field headquarters was raided and put out of action. Shortly afterward, the confusion was so great that the entire exercise was halted and the 77th was given orders to get out of the exercise and return to their base. For the next three weeks, the exercise went exactly as planned, but considerable ill feeling had been generated toward the Special Forces as a result of their operations.

It was perhaps unfortunate that the general who had been embarrassed by his field headquarters being overrun was the commanding general of Fort Bragg, and the senior officers of the 77th were waiting for some form of reprimand. What they expected did not occur, but when orders were issued that anyone in the Special Forces at Fort Bragg who was caught wearing a beret, or having one in his possession, would face a court-martial, everyone knew the reason: the general was having his day. Within the United States, away from Fort Bragg, the beret was worn with great caution, but it was still worn openly in the field by detachments on duty in Panama, Asia, and Germany.

Some two years after the banning of the beret at Fort Bragg, the general who issued the orders had the privilege to visit Bad Tolz. The commanding officer of the 10th Special Forces at that time was the ebullient, tough, intimidating Colonel Iron Mike Paulick. As he concluded his briefing on the 10th Special Forces to the visiting general, Iron Mike indulged in a tiny bit of theatrics that he bestowed on every official visitor to

Bad Tolz. He quickly placed a green beret, appropriately decorated with a major general's two stars, on the man's head.

The bewilderment, disgust, and rage on the general's face was incredible. Shaking with anger, he snatched the beret from his head and threw it across the room. Without saying a word he stormed out of the building, went straight to his staff car, and ordered his driver to get him out of Bad Tolz, where he was never seen again.

Whatever the general did to reprimand Iron Mike Paulick obviously did not affect his career, as he was later to rise to the rank of brigadier general.

The commanding general who did not like the beret, or the Special Forces, left Fort Bragg in 1960, but his orders remained in effect, and although almost every man in the 77th had a beret hidden away somewhere, it was simply not worth the risk to wear it within a hundred miles of the fort.

In 1961 President Kennedy visited Fort Bragg to review the Airborne Corps and the Special Forces. Being the junior, or orphan, unit, the Special Forces were virtually the last on the list for inspection, despite the fact that the President had developed a particular interest in unconventional warfare.

When the 77th's commanding officer, Colonel William Yarborough (later brigadier general), marched out to lead his men for the review, he surprised everyone. To the utter disbelief and joy of his men, and the horror of the generals and senior officers of the Airborne, Colonel Yarborough invited a court-martial: he was wearing a green beret.

President Kennedy immediately took to the colonel and spent a considerable amount of time with him discussing the training and use of the Special Forces. During that time Colonel Yarborough was also asked to explain the significance of his green beret, as the President had not failed to notice the reactions of those around him when Yarborough appeared. The colonel explained everything, particularly the fact that the beret was banned and that he had therefore left himself open to a court-martial.

Within hours of his return to Washington, President Kennedy sent a message to the Army stating that he considered the green beret of the Special Forces symbolic of one of the highest levels of courage and achievement in the history of the United States military.

It did not take much time for the Pentagon to respond to the Commander in Chief's message; a short time later, orders were issued authorizing the wearing of the green beret by the Army Special Forces.

President Kennedy was something of a student of Irish history. His decision to permit the wearing of the green beret perhaps was due in part to his feeling for his ancestral home; he most certainly knew some of the verses of the popular old Irish song bemoaning the ban on the wearing of the shamrock:

> For there's a cruel law agin
> The wearin' o' the Green!
> For they're hangin' men an' women
> There for wearin' o' the Green!

As for the practical value of the beret itself, any soldier, regardless of his nationality, who has had the privilege of wearing one will tell you that it's the most useless piece of field headgear ever devised and that it should be confined to the parade ground in mild, dry weather! The only thing worth fighting for is what the green beret symbolizes.

4

BATTLEFIELD LOG:
Bong Son, Vietnam—July, 1965

The guerrillas in the Vietcong regimental headquarters in the northeast sector of Binh Dinh province were taken completely by surprise when the 883rd Vietnamese Regional Force Company attacked.

The 883rd consisted of four platoons, each led by a U.S. Army Special Forces soldier. In over-all command, and also leading the first platoon, was Captain Paris Davis. Master Sergeant Billy Waugh led the second platoon, Staff Sergeant David Morgan led the third, and Specialist 4 (SP4) Brown led the fourth.

The company left their base camp near Bong Son under cover of darkness and moved stealthily through the hills and jungle toward the enemy headquarters. The actual raid commenced shortly after midnight, and everything went according to plan for the first few hours. When the first flare burst over the enemy stronghold, the men of the 883rd opened up with a fusillade of rifle and machine-gun fire that cut down dozens of Vietcong. By the time the enemy regained their composure and started to act in an organized manner, over one hundred of their men were dead, and Captain

Davis had called for an organized withdrawal of his forces.

Davis, like any other experienced leader of a commando-style raid, was well aware of the fact that an organized fighting withdrawal of a raiding force from behind enemy lines was one of the most important aspects of any guerrilla operation. Military records of almost all penetration raids into enemy-held territory clearly show that undetected infiltration and successful completion of the attack phase were relatively easy to accomplish—by comparison to the successful withdrawal of the raiding force.

The reasons for the difficulties encountered during attempts to effect a safe withdrawal of a raiding force are simple. The enemy, apart from being alerted, is usually angered by the fact that their territory has been violated. They are invariably infuriated that they were caught "off guard"; as a result, they become fanatical in their attempts to seek retribution for the deaths of their colleagues and the destruction caused by the raiders. Finally, they are very familiar with their surroundings and can move much faster, particularly at night, than can the withdrawing raiders, who have to make their escape either by returning via their infiltration route or navigating their way out through completely unfamiliar terrain.

Prior to the start of the raid, Captain Davis had posted security guards on the flanks and at the rear of the company so that the enemy could not mount a surprise flank attack, and to protect against the possibility of an attack by an enemy patrol returning from a mission. He had also posted extra guards along the banks of a fairly wide river that ran past the camp, as it would have allowed the enemy to outflank him much quicker than if they had to struggle through the jungle. When he ordered the entire company to break off the assault and withdraw, he signaled the security guards to pull back and join the remainder of the company.

As he was giving the order, his first platoon decided that they had no wish to be part of an organized withdrawal. The Vietnamese platoon officer, the noncommissioned officers, and almost all the soldiers had but one idea in their heads: to get as far away as fast as possible from the enraged enemy—regardless of the rest of the company. Those members of the platoon who had no such idea did what was natural—they simply followed their friends and colleagues.

At first Captain Davis thought that the platoon had just pulled back a little farther than he had ordered, so he started to search for them. When he finally realized that his platoon had in fact bolted, he was furious and immediately set off after them through the jungle.

Meanwhile, the remainder of the company, now under the command of Master Sergeant Waugh, were starting to conduct the withdrawal as planned. But the absence of the first platoon caused some confusion and concern among the Vietnamese of the remaining platoons. Waugh, Morgan, and Brown realized that the entire company was on the verge of running, and they quickly organized the remainder of the company to continue the withdrawal without the support of the first platoon.

As the company made its way out of the dense jungle surrounding the Vietcong camp into less-wooded areas, the enraged enemy pursued them relentlessly. When the attack had commenced on the enemy stronghold, the Vietcong had been driven into disarray, but as the assault progressed they had managed to organize themselves, despite the fact that they were taking a terrible beating, and they had sent out calls to their various outposts for help and reinforcements.

Although the reinforcements did not arrive before the raiders withdrew, they soon gave chase and caught up with the Vietnamese company. Other groups of Vietcong, mostly patrols returning to their regimental headquarters, either received word of the fleeing company or naturally migrated toward the running firefight and joined in the action.

It soon became obvious to Waugh that the enemy were growing in number and were starting to outflank his company. He drove his men as fast as he could, but the enemy appeared to have them almost completely surrounded, and the intensity of their fire was beginning to take effect. As the first streaks of dawn crept across the sky, Waugh discovered that his scouts had led the company into an open area that appeared to be surrounded by hundreds of the enemy.

He succeeded in organizing some of his men into a defensive position, despite the fact that the terrified Vietnamese soldiers were almost impossible to communicate with. As he set up his defensive position, enemy mortars started to fall; that created further terror among the men of the company and caused most of them to stop returning the enemy fire and to seek cover. Regrettably, a considerable number fled into nearby brush, shrub, and jungle.

Captain Davis finally managed to catch up with his fleeing men. As he made his way toward the front of the platoon, he heard a machine gun open up. The platoon, in its haste, had run straight into a Vietcong ambush. The enemy threw several grenades, and two of the platoon members were killed, while a few others, including Captain Davis, sustained minor injuries. Davis discovered that he had been hit on the back of his hand, but he paid no attention to the wound. He managed to get the runaway platoon reorganized, and, somewhat reluctantly, they started to follow him back toward the main group.

As he retraced his steps, Davis could hear the

sounds of the firefight in which Waugh, Morgan, and Brown were involved. He was carefully leading the platoon toward the action when a sudden noise ahead of them almost caused the men to turn tail again. A terrified Vietnamese came crashing along the trail. Just as Davis was about to cut him down, he recognized the man as one of the company.

The soldier explained that the remainder of the company were pinned down in an open field and taking heavy enemy fire. Davis persuaded him to lead them to the field and to remain with them when they arrived.

When he reached the company, Davis found them pinned down by heavy machine-gun and mortar fire behind a rough trench line in a small field. Most of the Vietnamese were huddled down and were not returning the fire. Waugh was in the middle of the field behind a small ditch and was busy engaging the enemy, SP4 Brown was lying close to another small ditch some distance to one side of him, and the immobile body of Sergeant Morgan lay near the edge of the field.

It was full daylight now. Davis ordered his platoon to return the enemy fire, but most of them ignored him and remained huddled behind the ditch. He moved up and down the ditch line firing at the enemy, shouting and cajoling the remains of the company to fire at the enemy. Some complied, but most did not.

As he moved along the line, a stream of machine-gun fire began to pour in from the right flank, killing several of the crouching Vietnamese soldiers. Davis made his way quickly to the flank and came face to face with five Vietcong climbing over the shallow ditch. A scathing burst from his M-16 killed all five. He returned to the center of the ditch line after persuading two of his terrified soldiers to guard the right flank.

As he was moving back to the center of the defensive line, he heard a burst of automatic-rifle fire coming from the left flank and made his way rapidly toward it.

The soldiers on the left flank were huddled behind a small ditch, rigid with fear. Six Vietcong were moving quickly toward the position. Davis pulled the pin from a fragmentation grenade and hurled it at them. The explosion felled four of the enemy, but the remaining pair continued their charge. Davis leveled his M-16 and squeezed the trigger. The result was a dull click instead of the powerful crack he expected. His immediate reaction was to change the magazine, but as soon as he removed the one on the weapon he realized it was not empty—the gun had jammed!

He quickly drew his pistol and shot one of the men as both came over the ditch. As the remaining enemy lunged at him, Davis swung his M-16, knocked him down, and clubbed him to death with the butt of the rifle.

As he cleared his jammed M-16, Davis saw Sergeant Morgan start to move, and moments later he saw dirt kicking up close to him. He called to Morgan and asked the extent of his injuries. The sergeant replied that as far as he could tell he was only slightly hurt; he could remember only the blast from an enemy mortar, and he believed that it had knocked him out. He was somewhat dizzy and could not quite see straight, but he knew that he was being shot at.

Davis yelled at Morgan to remain still, then started to look for the sniper, but he saw no further shots falling. As he was looking for the sniper, he heard Waugh yell that he had just been shot in the leg. Davis immediately leaped over the ditch and started across the field toward him, but he had only gone a few yards when a hail of automatic-rifle fire tore into the ground in front of him. He started to return the fire, but after another few yards several more enemy machine guns opened up and obliterated the ground in front of him. He scrambled back behind the ditch with a torrent of bullets close on his heels.

Davis quickly regained his breath and turned his attention to Master Sergeant Morgan, who had now recovered a little more and was again under fire from a sniper. Davis watched the dirt kick up close to the sergeant again and located the sniper in a heavily camouflaged foxhole. Moving closer to the enemy sniper's position, Davis took careful aim, squeezed the trigger, and instantly killed the sniper. He then crawled quickly over to the foxhole and discovered another two Vietcong struggling to get the body of the sniper out of the way. Davis pulled the pin of a grenade, let the firing lever fly off, and casually dropped the grenade into the hole. When it exploded, there was little doubt in his mind that the enemy were dead and buried.

Further enemy fire was swinging in the direction of Sergeant Morgan, who decided that the best course of action would be to remain as still as possible until there was a lull in the firing and he felt strong enough to get up. Davis agreed with him and went to his radio to try to get help.

Within a few minutes Captain Davis contacted a small Forward Air Control aircraft and explained his situation. The pilot, Captain Bronson, and his observer/navigator, Sergeant Ronald Dies, quickly located the beleaguered company's position and diverted a flight of Republic F-105 Thunderchief fighter bombers from a routine bombing mission. On instructions from Davis, Bronson fired his smoke rockets into the enemy positions and pulled away as the screaming supersonic fighter bombers swept in.

The first Thunderchief released its six and a half tons of bombs right on target, and the Vietcong decided to seek cover as they saw the second craft in the flight peel off and commence a bombing run.

The lull in the firing gave Davis the opportunity he had been waiting for. He raced out and helped Sergeant

Morgan to the comparative safety of the ditch. Once behind the ditch, Davis confirmed what Morgan had originally said—he was only slightly wounded and was suffering from shock more than anything else.

The last Thunderchief had dropped its bombs and pulled out of the area by the time Davis had taken care of Sergeant Morgan, at which time the enemy decided to mount another attack.

Incredibly, most of the remaining soldiers in the company would not fight back. Davis removed an M-60 machine gun from one of the terrified soldiers and brought it to bear on the charging enemy. He raked the line of scrambling Vietcong with the powerful machine gun and saw six of them pitch and contort as the 7.62-mm shells ripped into them. As they fell in a heap, their colleagues lost courage and fled. Davis lowered the M-60, spotted one of the company's 60-mm mortars, and immediately started to erect it.

As Davis was setting up the mortar, Morgan found that although he was still somewhat groggy, his eyesight at least had returned to normal. He picked up the M-60 machine gun, gathered up as much ammunition as he could find, and started to seek enemy targets.

Now that Davis had some support, he quickly finished setting up the mortar and gathered a stack of mortar rounds. He dropped five rounds down the tube in quick succession, and as they started to fall into the enemy positions, he leaped over the ditch and raced out toward Master Sergeant Waugh.

As Davis raced across the field, Morgan provided him with covering fire, and the enemy fire was considerably suppressed. However, although the enemy were obviously a little startled at the increased resistance they were receiving, the sight of Captain Davis brought renewed fire. Waugh had been hit four times in his lower leg and was very weak from both shock and loss of blood. Davis made several attempts to pick him up as

Special Forces Adviser S. Sgt. Howard Stevens (left) giving a last minute briefing to his Montagnard strike force. Vietnam, 1964.

Each member of this A Team has a specialty, but all are cross-trained to replace each other. As a twelve-man group, they go behind enemy lines and act as the nucleus of guerrilla activity. Fort Bragg, N.C., 1962.

A potential guerrilla leader learning the technique of rappelling (used to descend a sheer surface such as a cliff or building). Fort Bragg, N.C., 1961.

Advisers to a Vietnamese Special Forces battalion inspecting a machine gun at a perimeter defense position near Thoi Minh. Vietnam, 1964.

S.Sgt. Arthur Fletcher, a member of the U.S. Army Special Forces, helps two men of the Vietnamese Special Forces repair a 30-caliber machine gun. Vietnam, 1964.

Vietnamese trainees being supervised in firing M-79 grenade launchers. Camp Trai Trung Sup. Vietnam, 1967.

Training a Vietnamese in the operation of airboats for use during the monsoon season. Vietnam, 1966.

Sgt. Joseph McKnight, 5th Special Forces Group, laying a wire to a live Claymore mine for demonstration purposes. Fort Bragg, N.C., 1976.

Training at the Medical Field Service School in Houston, Texas, paratroopers jump from a C-119 aircraft known as the "Flying Boxcar."

Sfc. Evans Johnson, U.S. Army Special Forces adviser with over 23 years of Army service and over 1,000 parachute jumps. Vietnam, 1964.

U.S. Army Sgt. pushes his way through heavy undergrowth. Vietnam, 1964.

Member of 5th Special Forces Group mans a 30-caliber machine gun while Vietnamese Mobile Strike Force student pilots the boat. Vietnam, 1970.

Crossing an open rice field during a reconnaissance patrol, just after a two-hour Vietcong mortar attack. Vietnam, 1967.

Utilizing an improvised sand table, plans for a projected raid are explained during a training maneuver. Fort Bragg, N.C., 1962.

the enemy fire increased, but he just did not have the strength to do it. Waugh finally persuaded him to leave him where he was and to go back to the ditch where there was substantially more cover.

Racing back toward the ditch, Davis saw Morgan raking the enemy positions with heavy fire. He had almost reached the safety of the ditch when he felt a hot, searing pain in the back of his leg as an enemy bullet tore into his flesh. Once behind the ditch, he discovered that it was only a minor wound and he quickly regained his breath.

Davis went back to the radio to see if any reinforcements were on the way, and the Forward Air Controller informed him that it was being organized. Moments later, Captain Bronson called him to say that he had managed to get hold of a flight of McDonnell-Douglas F-4 Phantoms, each carrying over eight tons of mixed ordnance, and asked Davis for target designations.

With the aid of Sergeant Morgan, Captain Davis identified the enemy positions and called them back to Bronson. Shortly afterward, the tiny aircraft approached the area, fired a series of smoke rockets into the zone, and again pulled quickly away to one side. The first of the mighty Phantoms roared in and a searing blast of heat rent the air as its napalm bombs spread their jellied fire over the enemy positions.

As the second Phantom tore in with high-explosive bombs, Davis took off over the ditch toward the injured Master Sergeant Waugh. Sergeant Morgan again provided covering fire as Davis sprinted toward Waugh. As he bent down to pick up the wounded man, he felt another searing pain, this time in his wrist, and saw blood trickling down his hand. He ignored both the sensation and the sight of the blood, grabbed Waugh, and, with a surge of strength, hauled him up over his shoulder in a fireman's lift.

Davis staggered under Waugh's weight, but he managed to keep his balance as he slowly made his way back toward the ditch. The air around him was filled with the whistling and whining sound of enemy bullets, and he could see the ground in front of him being ripped apart by automatic-rifle fire. When he finally scrambled over the ditch, he was almost out of breath, but, incredibly, neither he nor the master sergeant had picked up any further injuries as they came through the gauntlet of enemy fire.

Morgan had more or less recovered from his state of shock and was now moving along the line, firing at the enemy and trying to persuade the remains of the terrified company to fight back. He was partially successful, managing to get a few more of them organized to help defend the position, but for the most part the men were not willing to fight.

Morgan was moving back from the right flank when a small group of enemy came scrambling over the ditch. He watched in horror as his own men dropped their guns and huddled down for safety. Before the screaming Vietcong could fire a shot, Morgan opened fire and wiped out the entire enemy group.

Captain Davis treated Waugh's injured leg as best he could, then went to see if he could get to SP4 Brown. Unfortunately, Brown was much farther away than Davis had at first thought, and he could not tell if Brown was alive or dead. When he realized that it would be suicidal to attempt to rescue Brown without considerable fire support, he immediately went to the radio and called for a medical evacuation helicopter for Waugh. He was informed that the helicopter was already on its way and that another Special Forces sergeant was also on board.

When the helicopter arrived, the pilot realized that he could not get his aircraft close to the company's

position—the enemy's fire was too intense. he informed
Davis that he could land some two hundred yards away
behind a small hill to effect the evacuation. Morgan
helped Davis sling the injured Master Sergeant Waugh
over his shoulder, then set out over the hill as Morgan
took charge of the feeble defense.

When the helicopter pilot saw Davis clear the top
of the hill he quickly dropped down to collect the
wounded man. As the aircraft landed, Sergeant First
Class Reinburg jumped off and ran down to assist
Morgan while Davis loaded Waugh into the helicopter.

Moments after Reinburg arrived at the defensive
position he was shot through the chest. He lay in an
open area that the enemy was saturating with fire.
Morgan and Davis were forced to dash out from cover
and drag him to safety where Davis administered first
aid.

The sight of the first helicopter must have convinced the Vietcong that they were about to lose their
prey, for they mounted a full assault on the ditch.
Davis, Morgan, and a few of the loyal Vietnamese met
the attack with grenades and rifle and machine-gun fire.
Morgan wiped out about fourteen of the enemy with
the M-60 machine gun, Davis took care of a further six
with his M-16 rifle and grenades, and the Vietnamese
soldiers killed eight or nine with rifle fire. The Vietcong
finally broke off the assault and went back into hiding.

An Army Command and Control helicopter with
an escort of Huey gunships arrived on the scene, and
the colonel on board ordered Davis to gather up his
remaining forces and leave.

Captain Davis protested, explaining that he had
one badly wounded American and another who he
thought might be alive but he could not get to him to
confirm it. When the colonel realized that Davis would
not pull out, he sent in another medical evacuation

helicopter to lift Reinburg out and ordered reinforcements sent in.

The sight of the evacuation helicopter caused the
enemy to mount another assault on the position. Davis,
Morgan, and a handful of the soldiers in the company
repulsed the attack, killing at least another twenty
Vietcong. All attempts to persuade the majority of the
company to fight failed, and the struggle continued
until mid-afternoon.

Two massive assaults were beaten back by the
small group of defenders, and the gunships used their
considerable firepower to stop several more from getting under way. The helicopter pilots would wait until
they saw the enemy start to gather behind their own
lines, or until Davis directed them to a particular area,
and then they would swing into action, weaving backward and forward across the enemy positions as they
poured down a great swath of machine-gun fire.

Despite the gunships' support, neither Davis nor
Morgan could get to Brown—his position was just too
exposed. It was not until troop reinforcements finally
arrived that Davis was able to get to him and drag him
to safety—some fourteen hours after the battle had
started.

The raid on the Vietcong regimental headquarters
was, without question, a complete success. However,
the withdrawal of the raiding party was—also without
question—a near disaster.

The incredible display of disloyalty by the men of
the 883rd Vietnamese Regional Force Company from
Bong Son was the prime cause of the catastrophic
withdrawal. Unfortunately, it was not an isolated incident; it had happened on several occasions in the past
with other companies, and it was one of the reasons
that compelled the Special Forces advisers to recruit

and employ the loyal Nung tribesmen from the northern parts of Vietnam as an "inner guard."

If there had been a platoon of Nungs involved in the battle near Camp Bong Son, the action would certainly not have ended so badly. However, it became obvious from the battle that the multiple talents and action of the Special Forces soldiers saved the entire company from being hunted down and wiped out by the Vietcong.

5

BATTLEFIELD LOG:
Freeman's Hollow, Vietnam—May, 1966

The Son Hai company of the Civilian Irregular Defense Group was based at the old French fort of Vinh Thanh in the south-central region of Binh Dinh province. The company consisted of about 115 men, most of whom were from the Rhade tribe of the Montagnards who inhabited the mountainous regions of Vietnam.

The mountain men were much smaller in stature than the inhabitants of the lowland and coastal regions of Vietnam, and they were affectionately known as "Yards" to the American troops beside whom they fought. (The nickname Yards was derived from the French word *Montagnards*, pronounced "Montanyards.")

The remainder of the Son Hai company were soldiers from the lowland areas and were usually referred to as "Vietnamese" by American military personnel in order to distinguish them from the Montagnards.

The camp had been opened, without much ceremony, on November 25, 1965, by three Montagnard companies, including the Son Hai company, and the Special Forces advisers of Detachment A-228 of the 5th

Special Forces Group. The old French defense system was rejuvenated and modified to incorporate the methods and structures that the Special Forces had discovered worked best for both the Montagnards and themselves against Vietcong attacks. The basic difference between the French and the Special Forces system was that the French had established the location as a small fort with almost all the defenses on the outer perimeter, whereas the Special Forces reestablished it as a fighting camp with an outer defense system that afforded clear fields of fire and a very secure inner defense system.

The inner complex was complete with underground bunkers and a command post designed to withstand intensive enemy mortar, rocket, and artillery fire, as well as prolonged attacks from determined assault troops who breached the outer defenses. The Special Forces advisers lived within this inner defense, for experience had unfortunately shown that although the Yards were extremely good fighters and were intensely loyal, a few were Vietcong infiltrators; these would invariably attempt to kill any Special Forces soldier they caught out in the open at night or who unwisely exposed himself during Vietcong attacks. The Vietnamese soldiers of the Civilian Irregular Defense Group presented much more of a problem—Vietcong sympathizers and infiltrators were a serious problem among their ranks. It was this problem that eventually forced the Special Forces to hire their own Nung soldiers.

The Montagnard soldiers, whose families always moved with them, and the Vietnamese of the Civilian Irregular Defense Force lived in the area between the inner and outer defense system; their primary responsibility was the defense of the outer perimeter. The Montagnard company commanders and the Vietnamese camp commander invariably established their own command posts outside the Special Forces inner defense system, and the entire defense and organization of the camp was under their jurisdiction.

As a result of intelligence gathered by a Special Forces reconnaissance patrol from the Vinh Thanh camp, the 1st Cavalry, which had over-all responsibility for the area, organized and launched "Operation Crazy Horse." This was an attempt to surround and wipe out a large group of Vietcong and their support elements from the regular North Vietnamese Army, in the mountainous area between the Song Ba and Soui Ca rivers north of the towns of An Khe and Phu Kat.

The Cavalry met with heavy resistance, but they managed to inflict serious damage on the Vietcong and were succeeding in their attempts to drive them out of the hills. By 0830 hours on May 26, most of the heavy fighting and battle action was over and the 1st Cavalry Division Commander, Major General John Norton, requested that the Son Hai company and its Special Forces advisers be inserted into the middle of the battle area.

Norton had a reasonable idea that a large force of Vietcong were still in the central mountain region northeast of Vinh Thanh, but he did not have the forces available within the Cavalry to confirm his suspicions, as he had them dispersed in a ring around the entire area in an attempt to seal it off. Although he did not intend to use the Special Forces–trained Civilian Irregular Defense Group company as an assault unit, he realized that inserting them into the area for reconnaissance and intelligence purposes could force them into the situation if they made contact with a large group of enemy.

He did not attempt to conceal that fact when he requested the use of the mostly Montagnard companies. The Yards agreed to conduct the operation if he promised to transport back to their own burial grounds the bodies of any soldiers killed in the area. Norton gave his word that this would be done and agreed also to provide air support and, if necessary, reinforcements should heavy fighting be encountered.

With those promises, the Yards looked forward to working, for the first time, as a regular component of the United States Army.

The insertion point in the mountains was a clearing officially named Landing Zone Monkey, and the first Huey transporter, called a "slick," to approach it carried a few members of the Son Hai company and two Special Forces sergeants, Burton Adams and Davis Freeman. (The transporters were called "slicks" because of their light armament, uncluttered appearance, and considerable speed.)

The Special Forces had been told that the landing zone was small and that it would have to be opened up and cleared by the advance party. As a result, a clearing team—a squad from A Company, 8th Engineer Battalion— under the command of Sergeant Turner Lawhorn, was on board the second Huey that would land in the clearing.

The pilot of the slick that carried Adams and Freeman knew the location of Landing Zone Monkey and wasted no time in getting to it. As he carefully maneuvered his craft down, both the Special Forces men became alarmed. The so-called clearing was at the bottom of a series of steep ridges alongside a small stream and was completely surrounded by jungle with trees more than fifty feet high. It was, as the Special Forces soldiers had been told, a natural clearing, but only because large slabs of rock and boulders that had fallen off the hillsides were strewn around in such a manner that they prevented any tree growth in the area. There was room for two helicopters to land, but only if the pilots exercised extreme caution.

Sergeant Freeman was the first off the helicopter

as the pilot hovered the craft some three feet from the
ground; he was quickly followed by Adams and the first
of the Yards, who spread out quickly to form a small
security ring. As the second slick, with the Engineer
demolition team on board, was touching down, Adams
and Freeman were conducting a quick survey of the
location. They both came to the same conclusions—it
was a dangerous landing site, difficult to protect, and
very exposed to innumerable firing positions from the
dense jungle on the steep hills that flanked it.

Their beliefs were confirmed when the third slick
approached. As the pilot tried to maneuver his craft
into the opening, the tail rotor came into contact with a
branch protruding from one of the taller trees. The
machine was over fifty feet from the bottom of the
clearing when it struck the tree. As it went out of
control it made a screaming noise like that of a large
wounded animal and plunged into the clearing. Adams,
Freeman, Lawhorn, and everyone else on the landing
zone barely managed to get out of the way as the great
whirling-blade contraption hit the ground.

With what little control he had, the pilot managed
to keep the machine in the clearing, but as it crashed,
he fractured his pelvis, and his copilot smashed his jaw.
Remarkably, the remainder of the crew, two door gunners, and the soldiers the aircraft was transporting were
just slightly shaken up, but they suffered no injuries.
The pilot and copilot were taken from the helicopter
and were treated by Sergeant Freeman, who was a
trained medic.

The landing zone was now completely blocked.
Sergeant Adams instructed the door gunners to strip
their M-60 machine guns and all other reusable compo-
nents off the wrecked craft. He then signaled the
remainder of the helicopters and ordered them to stay
away from the area until he could get the damaged craft
out of the way. With the assistance of Sergeant Lawhorn

and his engineers, the two gunners went to work stripping the aircraft, and in less than forty minutes they had a large pile of equipment stacked to one side of the landing zone.

Adams and Lawhorn then placed explosive charges in and around the helicopter to clear it from the landing zone. Both sergeants were well versed in demolition techniques, and when the charges were fired the helicopter was blown into pieces small enough to be manhandled out of the way. As the area was cleared, Adams signaled the fleet of slicks to bring in the remainder of the company.

By this time they had been in the clearing for almost two hours. Both Adams and Freeman knew that if there were any Vietcong in the vicinity, they would certainly have been alerted by either the crashing helicopter or the explosion it took to clear it. If their worst fears were correct, the enemy would now be moving toward the landing zone—in the form of either a reconnaissance patrol or an attack force. Both sergeants hoped that there would be no further trouble getting the remainder of the company into the clearing.

When the incoming slicks had landed sufficient troops to provide a reasonable defense force for the landing zone, Sergeant Freeman supervised the loading of the wounded pilots onto an evacuation helicopter, then instructed the two door gunners to load their salvaged equipment into another.

By 1000 hours the entire company had landed and small patrols had moved out a short distance from the clearing in order to extend the defensive ring.

When the last of the slicks departed the area, a relative calm descended on the landing zone and the two Special Forces sergeants relaxed a little. They had been expecting an attack before mid-morning—the Vietcong traditionally did not mount assaults during the hottest part of the day—and when it did not come by 1000 hours they were confident that they were reasonably safe.

The company, under the leadership of Commander Dimh Ghim and his assistant commander, Dinh Tach, was split into two groups. The majority of the company was organized into a fighting patrol, which set out on a reconnaissance mission. A platoon of Yards, under the command of Special Forces Sergeant Cecil Broome, was left at the landing zone to provide a defensive force to protect Sergeant Lawhorn and his Engineer squad as they opened up the clearing with explosives.

Although Sergeant Broome was the senior Special Forces soldier with the company, he was new to the country and quite unfamiliar with the customs and idiosyncrasies of the Yards, particularly when they were on patrol. Adams and Freeman had been instructed to operate with the company when they were in the jungle—they were old hands in the country and among the Rhade tribes of the Montagnards. Both men were trusted and respected by the leaders and the men of the Son Hai company, and they had reached that stage in their relationship with the Yards where they could have a heated argument, win their point, and still leave their opponents feeling that their honor and dignity had not been compromised—a vital requirement when dealing with most Asian races and not one that is easy to learn.

The reconnaissance patrol moved out of the bright light of the clearing into the half-light of the dense jungle and started to work their way slowly up the ridge to the north and west of the landing zone. With a squad of men at point, some forty or fifty yards ahead of the main group, the patrol moved cautiously in a single file along a rough jungle trail.

As the patrol moved up the mountainside, both Adams and Freeman were pleased to see that their

Rhade soldiers were taking great care to move quietly; on numerous occasions in the past they had been rather noisy. As they moved upward from the clearing, the nature of the jungle started to change and they encountered considerably more bamboo thickets. This did not hamper their progress much, since the trail they were following continued upward through the bamboo region—an almost certain indication that the enemy had been using the area.

Shortly after 1100 hours, they reached the crest of the ridge, which was almost one thousand feet higher than the landing zone, and immediately set up a defense position. During a short rest period, Freeman established radio contact with their camp at Vinh Thanh and reported their location and the events at the landing zone. After the rest period, Adams accompanied the company's Yard reconnaissance platoon, under the leadership of the assistant commander, Dinh Tach, who set out along the ridge crest to continue the reconnaissance mission.

The top of the ridge was shrouded with bamboo thicket, but the narrow trail they had followed opened up considerably and was quite well worn. The wider trail did not run along the very top of the ridge; it ran parallel to it just a short way down the slope and was fairly well concealed by the bamboo trees. The discovery of the wider and obviously more well-used trail produced a considerable amount of caution in the reconnaissance platoon, and they moved very quickly and quietly along the ridge. After about ten minutes they had covered almost three hundred yards. As they approached a small cross-trail, the point soldier signaled that he had detected a noise and some movement ahead.

The platoon rapidly disappeared from the trail into the thicket and prepared for an ambush as the men of the point squad, which included Sergeant Adams, strained their ears and eyes in the direction of the noise. In less than a minute a lone Vietcong came out of one of the side trails. He was armed with an AK-47 automatic rifle and was carrying six canteens that were obviously full of water. As he stepped onto the main trail, Adams hoped that his eager Yards, who were always tempted to start a fight the moment they spotted the enemy, would not try to gun the man down or take him prisoner.

The Vietcong looked back along the trail in the direction of the platoon, then casually turned and proceeded in the opposite direction. Adams held his breath. If the Yards were going to be foolish enough to gun the man down, they would do it at any moment. He was greatly relieved as the seconds ticked away and no shot was fired. Moments later, Dinh Tach, who was also with the point squad, signaled the platoon to withdraw, and the entire platoon moved quickly back along the trail toward the defense position and the remainder of the company.

When the company commander, Dimh Ghim, heard that the trail along the ridge had widened and that the Vietcong had been carrying six canteens, he became very excited. He assumed that there was a large group of the enemy somewhere nearby, and he wanted to throw the whole company into the fray immediately. His assistant, Dinh Tach, supported him on this plan, but the two Special Forces sergeants vehemently opposed it.

After considerable discussion, most of which was heated, Freeman and Adams persuaded the commander to change his mind about committing almost the entire company. Adams suggested that he and Freeman, along with twenty men, should conduct a further reconnaissance patrol to determine the size of the enemy group, and that the remainder of the company should try to fortify the defense position while they were gone.

Dimh Ghim, who was infinitely more eager to get into a fight than were the fierce little Yards of his company, was finally convinced that Adams's plan was the better of the two. But he would agree to it only if he was allowed to accompany Adams and Freeman on the patrol. They were against that idea, too, but Adams and Freeman did not put up much of a fight—it was obviously the only way Ghim would allow another reconnaissance patrol. Dinh Tach was left in command of the remainder of the company as the reconnaissance patrol set out.

This time it was decided that the trail itself would not be used. They split up into three small teams to work their way through the bamboo thickets, which were less dense than usual, on either side of the trail. Dimh Ghim led his team along the left side of the trail, Freeman took the right side on the sloping ground toward the top of the ridge, and Adams took the center, very close to the edge of the trail. They moved slowly forward from the defense position. After about fifteen minutes, they had progressed no more than seventy yards when Adams's group was subjected to a hail of automatic fire from extremely close range.

As the first torrent of bullets whined and crackled through the bamboo, Adams was hit in the back. The bullet slammed straight into his rucksack and, fortunately, was thereby prevented from going straight through his back. The force of the impact spun him around, and a second bullet tore with incredible force into his right arm and smashed it. As the impact hurled him to the ground, a further hail of fire screamed over his body; he would certainly have been killed if he had been standing up. The remaining members of his team were unhurt and immediately charged into the bamboo to get at the enemy.

Ghim's and Freeman's groups moved quickly forward and discovered that the enemy was well established in rows of bunkers covering about forty yards of the sloping ground on the side of the trail. During the next thirty-five minutes a fierce firefight ensued, and Freeman was extremely busy as the three small teams got together and assaulted the enemy positions.

Back at the defense position, Dinh Tach ordered almost all of the remainder of the company forward to assist the patrol. As they carefully made their way forward they came across the wounded Adams, who, although suffering badly from shock, was carefully crawling back along the edge of the trail carrying his weapon in his left hand.

The Yards in the patrol, accompanied by Freeman and Ghim, closed on the enemy in a series of overlapping moves. Ghim, carrying a Browning automatic rifle, was in the thick of the fight and used the heavy weapon with considerable effect to keep the enemy pinned down as his men moved slowly forward. Freeman used his M-16 with great accuracy and within the first fifteen minutes killed two of the enemy.

The small patrol closed on the enemy positions after about twenty-five minutes, when they were starting to receive assistance from the covering fire from the first elements of the company that had arrived from the defense position. Freeman killed a further two enemy snipers with his M-16, and in a final flurry of grenades, Browning automatic rifle fire, and M-14s, the patrol drove the enemy out of their bunkers.

When the assault was over, one 7.62-mm machine gun and seven AK-47 rifles were captured, and fifteen enemy bodies were counted. A considerable number of the enemy who fled were known to have been wounded, for numerous trails of blood were discovered around the location.

Three of the Yard patrol were dead, eight were

wounded in addition to Sergeant Adams, and no weapons were missing. Freeman treated the wounded as the patrol and the forward elements of the company slowly pulled back toward the defense perimeter. Meanwhile the enemy regrouped and moved back in to snipe at them as they withdrew, but it was obvious that they had been badly shaken by the assault on their positions, since they made no attempt to openly challenge the withdrawal. However, intense sniping from the surrounding area continued throughout the entire withdrawal, despite the fact that the distance covered was only about seventy yards. Fortunately, the company sustained no further injuries as they made their way back along the ridge.

Once back in their defense position on top of the ridge, the company tightened the perimeter as Freeman continued to administer medical treatment to Adams and the other wounded. Although Adams was still mobile, he was effectively out of action since he was still suffering from shock and was in acute pain, despite the morphine that he had been given. Freeman was now in charge of the operation. Although he felt that the Vietcong they had just engaged were not a large force, and that the company had inflicted considerable damage on them, he believed that a further show of force was required.

He contacted the Tactical Operations Center, which was based at Landing Zone Savoy to the south of the Special Forces base camp at Vinh Thanh, and requested an air strike on the ridge. He gave the operations center the coordinates for the strike, carefully checking them on his map as he called them out, and was advised that the aircraft would be there within ten minutes. He would have preferred to use the artillery, as he knew he could have "walked" the guns backward and forward across the ridge with remarkable accuracy. However, he did not call for it; he knew the Yards were terrified of artillery barrages, either enemy or friendly, and would simply get up and bolt if even friendly guns started to drop their shells too close.

The Yards' fear was based on a simple premise: first, the artillery gunners could not see what they were shooting at and therefore it was dangerous; second, because the Yards could not see the guns firing, they had no idea in which direction to look. No amount of explanation about the accuracy of modern artillery could convince them, and the occasional short round that occasionally fell too close to a friendly position served only to close their minds further. They could tolerate air strikes, as they could see the attacking aircraft, and they had a half-belief that the pilots could see them or at least their position, which of course was definitely not the case; the pilots were invariably bombing on coordinates or on smoke markers only.

The Forward Air Control aircraft arrived over the ridge at about 1155 hours, shortly after Freeman had placed his request, and made contact with the company. Freeman confirmed the location for the strike, and a few minutes later the attack aircraft arrived and saturated the ridge with high explosives. As the bombing was taking place, the Yards displayed a form of nervousness more usually seen in thoroughbred racing horses.

Suddenly, one five-hundred-pound bomb strayed from the target area, plunged into the ground within fifty yards of the defense position, and exploded. The ridge vibrated and shook, and the company was showered with dirt, stones, and shattered bamboo. Freeman heard the teeth of at least fifty men chattering and watched the tiny mountain men prepare to bolt if just one more bomb came that close.

The air strike finished without any more near misses. From the damage that had been done and the fact that they were not being sniped at, Freeman reckoned that at least a few more enemy had been destroyed. He again called the Tactical Operations Center and requested helicopter evacuation for the dead and wounded from the top of the hill. A large twin-rotor CH-47 Chinook was promised if he could prepare a landing site on top of the hill. Freeman replied that he would have one ready in about an hour, as he had no wish to return to Landing Zone Monkey for the evacuation. He considered it a death trap.

When he had finished talking to the operations center, Freeman called Sergeant Lawhorn down at Monkey and instructed him to bring his entire Engineer team up to the ridge to prepare another landing zone. Lawhorn, who disliked Landing Zone Monkey as much as Freeman did, wasted no time—within thirty minutes he and his team were on the ridge. Lawhorn selected a suitable area and within twenty-five minutes enough jungle trees and bamboo had been blasted away to permit the Chinook to land.

The men heard the giant helicopter long before they saw it. But when they eventually spotted it they were disappointed, as the pilot was searching another ridge several miles away. They watched in frustration as the helicopter wandered about from ridge to ridge and moved farther away. Freeman tried to relay messages through the operations center, but the pilot still could not locate them. Finally, the pilot decided that he did not have sufficient fuel to continue his search and returned to his base. For a brief period of time he became the most cursed pilot ever to set foot in a Chinook.

The Tactical Operations Center called back and ordered Freeman to take the entire company back down into Landing Zone Monkey, where Huey pilots who knew the area would fly in to evacuate the wounded and the dead. Freeman, the wounded Adams, and Lawhorn protested vehemently, stating that if the enemy were gathering forces to attack them, Monkey was the worst place to invite a firefight. Their pleas were not heard and the orders were reiterated: "Return to Lima-Zulu Monkey." Somewhat disgruntled, yet happy at the fight they had put up against the Vietcong, the company, carrying their wounded and dead, moved back down the narrow trail to the rocky landing zone.

As they moved down the trail, Freeman organized a rear guard party in the event that the enemy had organized themselves to snipe at the rear of the company, although he did not expect it, as there had not been a single shot fired in their direction since the air strike.

6

BATTLEFIELD LOG:
Freeman's Hollow, Vietnam (Part Two)—May, 1966

The Son Hai company reached the boulder-strewn hollow without incident, but the rear guard reported to Freeman that they had the impression they had been followed all the way down. Freeman sent a small patrol to watch the trail some fifty yards from the landing zone.

The security party, under Sergeant Broome, had done little to organize the area in the absence of the remainder of the company. This did not surprise Adams or Freeman, who knew that the Yards and the Vietnamese had not yet accepted Broome and that he was having difficulty communicating with them. It was something that only time among the tribesmen would cure.

Once back at the landing zone, the company set up a defense perimeter and settled down to have lunch. Freeman, who was very uneasy about the surroundings, continually checked on the wounded, and hoped that the evacuation helicopters would arrive soon.

Shortly after 1330 hours, the first of the helicopters appeared and landed in the clearing. On board the slick were three men. Among them was Lieutenant Walker, a Special Forces officer who immediately took command, as he had been instructed to hold the company in the hollow until further orders were received. The second man was Sergeant Alan Arrowsmith from Headquarters Company, 1st Brigade, Cavalry Division. Arrowsmith, like a considerable number of people in the Headquarters Division, had assumed that all the fighting was over and had come to Landing Zone Monkey simply out of curiosity, as he wanted to see how the Special Forces soldiers operated with the Montagnards; he was also prepared to assist in any manner he could. The third man was Lieutenant Wade Hathaway, an artillery forward observer who had been sent in to coordinate any artillery strikes that might be called.

At about 1400 hours, after the wounded and dead were lifted out, Lieutenant Walker sent Sergeant Broome back up the ridge trail with a platooon of Yards. Broome was instructed to send Freeman's small squad back to the clearing and to set the platoon up in an ambush position about 150 yards from the hollow. Walker instructed him to return to the clearing when this was done.

Freeman was once again third in the Special Forces chain of command, a position he quite easily accepted, but his tactical mind was still working. He carefully talked to Dimh Ghim, suggesting that perhaps a better defense perimeter could be set up. Ghim completely agreed with him, and the two men set about reorganizing and repositioning the soldiers into safer, more secure positions. As they were doing this, Sergeant Broome returned from the trail and quietly joined them.

Meanwhile, Sergeant Lawhorn's Engineers, a squad of tireless workers, set about organizing the zone and establishing a log bunker and better fighting holes. The visitor, Sergeant Arrowsmith, did not interfere; he busied himself taking photographs and watching and listening to the Special Forces soldiers.

Relative calm had descended on the company as the afternoon progressed, but it was broken at 1630 hours by the unscheduled arrival of a single slick. The pilot landed quickly and smoothly, and the crew immediately started to unload cases of ammunition and mortar rounds. An ammunition resupply had not been called for, and, in one of those rare battlefield situations, a resupply upset the troops.

There were now an extra two hundred rounds of ammunition for each man and one hundred more shells for their one and only 60-mm mortar. The Yards did not want the ammunition; they wanted to be as mobile as possible, as they were well aware that mobility in such an environment was a lifesaver. Two hundred rounds of ammunition is a considerable amount of extra weight, particularly for men of such small stature, and one hundred extra rounds of high-explosive mortar shells, weighing almost three pounds each, did not help the situation.

The Yards, like Sergeant Freeman, did not like Landing Zone Monkey. They wanted to get away from it as quickly as possible and they saw the extra ammunition as a problem. They did not want to carry it, and they knew that it could not be left at the location, but they did not want to be forced into a situation where they had to stay and guard it. They wanted to fire it off into the jungle to get rid of it.

Lieutenant Walker agreed to the extra mortar shells being fired off into the area on top of the ridge where the company had contacted the enemy, but he insisted that each man take his share of the remainder of the ammunition, since they would not be resupplied for several days. Grudgingly, the Yards accepted this and set about firing the mortar rounds.

Out of the first eighteen rounds there were eleven misfires. It was quickly discovered that the mortar itself was working perfectly, as the rounds were dropping on the striker at the base of the barrel and the firing mechanism of the mortar was functioning. The problem was clearly with the batch of shells they had just received.

A misfire with a mortar is not like a misfire with a rifle. In the first place, the mortar round is loaded with a propellant charge and a high-explosive charge, and it is in a fully armed condition when it drops to the bottom of the mortar barrel. If the propellant charge does not ignite when the ignition cartridge hits the striker at the bottom of the barrel, a dangerous and nerve-racking situation results. The armed round, with its misfired propellant charge, sits at the bottom of the vertically pointing barrel and can be removed only by laying the barrel over on its side and very gently shaking the round out. If the propellant charge should suddenly ignite during this procedure, the result can be catastrophic—the launching tube would get hurled backward with incredible force, and the high-explosive mortar round would more than likely impact and explode within the immediate area.

One misfire of a mortar is usually enough to fray a few nerves, but eleven misfires in a short period of time really tore at the nerves of the Yards, as well as the nerves of the Special Forces soldiers. Lieutenant Walker, on the advice of Sergeants Freeman and Lawhorn, decided that the entire batch of mortar rounds was in such a dangerous condition that the best course of action was to blow it all up.

Sergeant Lawhorn's tireless Engineer squad dug a deep pit at the edge of the clearing, and all the misfired and untried mortar rounds were carefully placed at the bottom. Lawhorn attached a small explosive charge to the rounds and was preparing to set it off when an incredible little scene developed.

The Yards had by now stretched both their nerves and their patience to the limit, and Freeman knew that something was going to give. The men's reaction to the decision to blow up the suspect mortar rounds did not surprise or upset him, as he fully understood their thinking. They were still upset at having to carry the extra ammunition, and if the mortar rounds were to be destroyed they could see no reason why the extra ammunition should not be destroyed with it. Besides, they reasoned, if the mortar rounds were bad, there was every likelihood that the ammunition was also bad. The thought of their precious rifles misfiring in the middle of a firefight was a foreboding one and it fueled their determination to get rid of the ammunition.

With the support of their commander, Dimh Ghim, the men started to dump their extra ammunition into the pit. Lieutenant Walker was highly annoyed, and a heated argument ensued between the two men as groups of Yards continued to throw their extra magazines into the pit. When Lawhorn had everything ready, he sat behind a large rock, ready to fire the charge whenever Walker gave the order. Sergeant Arrowsmith and the forward observer, Lieutenant Hathaway, were close by, and Broome was standing beside Walker as the argument continued. Freeman was farthest away; he was busy ensuring that the defenses were being manned.

The assistant commander of the company, Dinh Tach, took sides with Walker and proceeded to drag his men over to the pit and force them to retrieve their ammunition. Dinh Tach, who was the biggest and strongest of all the Yards, was silent but persuasive, and the ammunition was slowly being retrieved from the pit as the row between Walker and Dimh Ghim became more heated.

The cracking and popping sound of automatic-rifle fire coming from the jungle ended the argument. Everyone took cover, but they soon realized that the shooting was not directed at them. Sergeant Broome raced from the clearing and up the trail, Freeman quickly checked the perimeter defenses, and everyone else sought suitable cover as the sound of a firefight in the jungle continued. Broome was back within a few minutes with word that the ambush platoon were being attacked from three sides and were fighting their way back to the clearing. Walker ordered Lawhorn not to fire the charge in the pit, and as he did so a hail of rifle and machine-gun fire poured into the landing zone from three directions.

Almost every man in the company immediately opened fire into the jungle, despite the fact that they could not see the enemy. When Freeman could not hear any further enemy fire coming into the zone, he called a halt to the counterfire. After almost two minutes of silence, the area was again saturated with machine-gun fire, but this time it came from the jungle around the trail. Moments later it was joined by a tremendous stream of fire from the same areas as the previous fire. As rifle and machine-gun bullets whined and ricocheted off the rocks and boulders in the landing zone, everyone realized that they were now surrounded. The entire company again opened fire into the jungle at an enemy they could not see, and after a few minutes of heavy counterfire from the Yards the attack stopped.

There was no firing for nearly five minutes, and it seemed that the enemy attack had been repulsed. A few of the Yards were standing up and moving around, as were Sergeant Broome and Lieutenant Walker. Walker was on the radio to the Tactical Operations Center at Landing Zone Savoy, requesting that the rocket-carrying aerial artillery Hueys be sent in to strike the entire area around the clearing.

Freeman, who did not think that the enemy had given up, finished bandaging a slightly wounded soldier and remained in his defense position. He called to the Yards who were moving around and told them to keep their heads down; they obeyed, with replies of "Yes, Doc" and "Okay, Doc," which was the way they always addressed him.

As if to emphasize his warning, a few shots were fired into the landing zone from different directions, confirming Freeman's suspicions that the enemy had not left. The enemy snipers were now going to harass them until another major attack was launched—a typical Vietcong Tactic. Sergeant Broome and Lieutenant Walker were still in the open as the random bullets whined and skidded off rocks.

Freeman heard a sharp crack from somewhere behind him and, at the same time, felt and heard a bullet whistle past his head. The bullet hit Broome in the back just beneath his left shoulder blade. Broome gasped, staggered for a moment, and fell over. Less than two seconds after he heard and felt the first shot, Freeman was subjected to a repeat performance; the second bullet hit Lieutenant Walker on the right side of his face and came straight out through his lower jaw.

Sergeant Arrowsmith, who had wisely taken cover in a crevice between two boulders, pulled out his first-aid package and started to crawl toward the fallen men. Freeman yelled at him to get back under cover and moved quickly toward Broome. As soon as he reached Broome he realized the man was dead. Freeman then moved over to Lieutenant Walker, who had slumped down by the radio.

Arrowsmith watched in fascination as Freeman calmly knelt in the open for almost ten minutes, carefully giving the lieutenant an injection of morphine and bandaging his face. As he worked in his exposed position, bullets thudded into the ground beside him and kicked up the dirt and dust, but Freeman paid no attention. However, as he worked on Walker, a nagging thought kept crossing his mind.

Broome and Walker had been shot by the same sniper, who was obviously still in the nearby jungle. Both bullets had passed within a foot of Freeman's head, and from the cracking sound of the gun that had fired the bullets, he knew that the sniper was very, very close—perhaps even within the defense perimeter. Freeman, like most good soldiers, could easily distinguish the difference between the sound of an enemy weapon and that of a friendly one, which varies mostly because of the difference in ammunition. The shots Freeman had heard were not exactly those of a standard enemy weapon, and although he was well aware that the Vietcong did use captured M-14s and M-16s, he did not like the implication. But he realized that he had to accept the possibility that it was one of their own men, and his fears seemed to be justified by virtue of the fact that the sniper could easily have shot him first; he certainly had plenty of opportunity to do so as he knelt there treating Walker.

When Freeman finished treating Walker, he signaled to Arrowsmith to come and help him. They carried Walker over to the edge of the clearing and placed him behind a pile of felled trees. Because of his experience and his command of the Yards, Freeman realized that he was once again responsible for the entire operation, despite the fact that he was outranked by several men on the landing zone. The fire from the jungle into the landing zone was steadily increasing and hand grenades were now being thrown by the enemy.

Freeman immediately called the Tactical Operations Center and explained the situation. He requested reinforcements as he estimated that they were being attacked by at least two enemy companies. The operations center had become alarmed when Walker called for the rocket ships and had informed General Norton. He had immediately ordered reinforcements to be sent, and men of B Company, 8th Cavalry Regiment were already airborne when Freeman called and requested them.

It was getting late in the day and Freeman knew that the reinforcements would only just get there before dark. He sent Arrowsmith to find Lieutenant Hathaway just as the enemy hurled another shower of grenades into the rocks and increased their fire. The pattern of the attacks now convinced Freeman that they were not fighting just Vietcong—they were up against some regular units from the North Vietnamese Army.

By the time Arrowsmith crawled back with Lieutenant Hathaway, the enemy had brought a mortar into action, but the crew seemed to be having difficulty finding the range. The Son Hai company mortar was not in use, as no discernible target could be found for it; in any case, Freeman doubted if the Yards would operate it after the incident with the dud rounds.

Freeman asked Hathaway to direct the attack of the rocket-firing Hueys of the aerial artillery when they arrived overhead. He also asked him to call up the 155-mm guns at the fire base near Landing Zone Cobra, which was located some distance to the south of the Special Forces camp at Vinh Thanh, and to request them to stand by to provide further bombardment when the rocket ships had finished. Hathaway liked the way the sergeant was thinking.

The firefight had increased in intensity by the time the first slick carrying the reinforcements from B Company arrived. Despite the fact that a firefight was obviously in progress, the pilot of the first helicopter committed himself to getting down to the landing zone. Freeman called for maximum counterfire as the helicopter started to drop into the clearing and everyone responded. As the helicopter dropped toward the land-ing zone, the door gunners on either side of the craft blasted away at the nearby jungle.

The pilot brought the craft to a hover some three feet off the ground, and five infantrymen, led by Ser-geant Kenneth Wells, leaped out and dived for cover in a hail of enemy fire. The helicopter pilot pulled pitch as fast as he dared and swept his machine up and out of the clearing, thankful that the sergeant and his men had not delayed their departure from the craft.

As the first slick cleared the area, the second helicopter, piloted by Chief Warrant Officer Francisco Moreno, approached the clearing. He warned his crew on the intercom that he was going to attempt to get down. The door gunners, Staff Sergeant Herbert McDuffy and Specialist 4 Angel Cumba, flicked off the safeties on the M-60s and opened fire as Moreno swung over the clearing. The six riflemen passengers on board the slick did not have to be told to prepare themselves to get out of the craft as fast as possible when it got close to the ground.

When they were still some fifty feet in the air, a burst of automatic fire from the jungle tore through the left side of the helicopter toward the rear of the engine compartment. The impact was not felt by anyone on board, but the damage to the hydraulic system was immediately registered on the instruments in front of Moreno. He calmly told his crew that he was losing power and would have to set the craft on the ground. Moreno picked the best spot he could, and as he slowed the descent to a slight hover close to the ground, the riflemen, who knew nothing of the mechanical problem, leaped out of the craft and sought cover.

Moreno, now certain that the crash landing would be gentle, automatically cut the power, switched off the fuel supply, and fired the automatic fire extinguishers on the engine. As he was doing this, McDuffy and

Cumba were still blazing away at the jungle with their M-60s. With Moreno's skillful handling, the helicopter hit the ground with just a gentle bump. McDuffy and Cumba immediately lifted the M-60s off their mounts and leaped out. Disregarding their own safety, they opened the pilot's door and provided covering fire as Moreno and his copilot got out of the stricken craft.

Moreno was surprised that Freeman was in command, but within seconds of getting to him he realized why. His resolute calm as he directed the firefight, while at the same time attending the wounded men amid a storm of enemy bullets, grenades, and mortars, deeply impressed Moreno. Freeman found him an M-16, as pilots were armed with only a .38 pistol, and directed him, along with the rest of his crew, to a defense position.

With one helicopter effectively blocking the middle of the clearing and the intense enemy fire, it became obvious to Freeman that any attempt to bring the others in would be inviting more trouble. As he radioed them to pull away, the rocket-carrying Hueys called to inform him that they would arrive in about twenty minutes. Freeman gave the handset to Lieutenant Hathaway to bring them in.

About ten minutes before the rocket ships arrived, enemy firing ceased and Freeman took the opportunity to move around the defenses to see to the wounded. As he did so, he spent a little time with the remainder of the defenders, reorganizing and encouraging them. The casualty list was rising in the hollow, but Freeman was certain that the enemy was not getting away unscathed.

It was almost dusk when the rocketeers arrived and, under the expert guidance of Hathaway, blasted the entire area around the landing zone with a remarkable display of firepower and accuracy. As they pulled away, Freeman was convinced that if the enemy had been preparing to attack as darkness fell, they must certainly have been persuaded against it. However, taking no chances, he signaled Hathaway to bring in the guns.

Freeman warned the Yards that artillery was on the way—he did not want them to bolt or to freeze up at its unexpected arrival. The rocket-firing Hueys had not worried them, and Freeman was certain that by now they could take a little artillery.

Hathaway and the 155-mm gunners knew their job, and the first white phosphorous shell came ripping through the air to fall well clear of the zone. As the white smoke rose in the fading light, Hathaway called a few minor corrections and an impressive barrage was walked up and down the trail leading to the ridge for over thirty minutes.

As the barrage finished, Freeman asked Arrowsmith to gather all the Americans at the south end of the hollow. The memory of the shots that had killed Sergeant Broome and wounded Lieutenant Walker were still fresh in Freeman's mind. He trusted the Yards, but he knew he could not do so blindly. He was now convinced that the sniper, who had been only a few feet away from him when the incident occurred, was one of the company.

There were twenty-two Americans in the hollow and Freeman explained that he wanted them to form a small inner defense ring at the edge of the landing zone close to the stream. He told them that as night fell the Vietcong and the regular North Vietnamese Army unit that he was now certain were out there would definitely launch an attack. He explained that although he trusted his Yards and the few Vietnamese that were with them, the enemy would certainly try to infiltrate during the night and attempt to convince them to surrender. The Vietcong would promise to let the Yards and Vietnamese go free if they would leave the Americans to them—it had happened before, with disastrous results.

Freeman further explained that even if that did not happen, there was still the possibility that a massive attack would be launched and the landing zone might be overrun. If that seemed likely, he wanted the Americans to be together so that he could lead them in a fighting withdrawal out of the hollow and up the slope of the ridge, where he knew he could organize a better defense. Freeman did not mention his concern over the incident involving Broome and Walker.

Everyone agreed with him and a tight inner defense ring of Americans was quickly established under Freeman's supervision. It had no sooner been done than the enemy mounted another attack and swept the zone with automatic fire. In the middle of the firefight, Freeman was called to the radio. The Tactical Operations Center informed him that an Air Commando AC-47 Spooky gunship was almost at the location, accompanied by a flare ship, and that they would be available to him throughout the night, either on station directly overhead or in the vicinity. Freeman welcomed the news and immediately contacted the aircraft.

As the first series of flares bathed the landing zone with their eerie light, the enemy stopped firing. The gunship pilot fired a short burst for Freeman to confirm the line of fire, then proceeded to lay down an incredible swath of fire from the aircraft's three side-firing miniguns. That appeared to deter the enemy, as they did not continue the attack when the flares burned out.

Throughout the night there was sporadic sniper fire, and occasionally the flare ship lit the area just to keep the enemy thinking. Freeman ordered the Yards not to fire unless they could see a live target; he was expecting the enemy to attack just after dawn and he did not want to waste ammunition, which was now getting dangerously low. In anticipation of the dawn attack, he asked Hathaway to arrange for the aerial artillery helicopters to be on station for dawn and for the 155-mm guns to take over the bombardment when the rocketeers had finished.

Freeman moved only twice during the night: he took care of the wounded and, as dawn approached, he carefully checked the defenses. The first rays of light brought the rocket ships, which again followed Hathaway's instructions and laid down an incredibly accurate barrage of screaming and whistling high-explosive projectiles. When they had expended their rocket launchers, the Hueys pulled away and Hathaway brought the guns in. Once again they were on target with their first round and they plastered the slopes as Hathaway directed.

Thirty minutes of near silence ensued after the barrage had finished, and Freeman knew that the enemy had been driven off. He sent patrols out a short distance from the clearing and they counted thirty-seven bodies, all of them regular North Vietnamese Army soldiers. Trails of blood in almost every direction gave some indication of the casualties that had been inflicted on the enemy, and the Son Hai company was delighted that the battle was over.

The first Med Evac (Medical Evacuation) Huey arrived at 0700 hours, and throughout the morning a steady stream of helicopters flowed in and out of the landing zone, the largest of which was the huge helicopter known as the "flying crane" that lifted Moreno's damaged helicopter out of the hollow in one piece.

As the slick carrying the last of the Americans out of Landing Zone Monkey lifted off, someone remarked that they ought to rename the place "Freeman's Hollow." Freeman had no comment—he did not like the place when he had first set eyes on it, and as he was leaving he still did not like it. His tactical mind could not be compromised—a jungle clearing at the bottom of a hollow could never by anything but a lousy place to fight from.

7
CONCEPTS AND ISSUES

The general public has apparently been almost completely misled by the news media and the motion-picture industry regarding the exact role of the Special Forces.

The Army Special Forces are not commandos, storm troopers, assault troops, raiders, jungle fighters, or some type of elite parachute regiment similar to the Rangers. They are not the Army equivalent of the Navy SEALs, Air Force Commandos, or Marine Reconnaissance Units, nor are they some sort of militiary intelligence organization.

They are, simply stated, highly qualified *teachers* of specialized military fighting skills and of the art of living and surviving under adverse and primitive conditions. Despite the fact that all operational engagements related in this book show them in a fighting role, they are actually still functioning as teachers during the conduct of practical field operations.

The primary mission role of the Special Forces, in 1985, can be defined as the education of the forces of less sophisticated, friendly nations in methods of defense, by teaching them how to conduct either conventional or unconventional warfare.

The task of teaching conventional military skills appears to have been added to the Special Forces role, along with various other tasks, when it was realized that the training they received for their unconventional-warfare role automatically qualified them for much more. When the Army generals realized that they had a source of multitalented, multilingual, mature, and professionally experienced warriors in the Special Forces, they started to use them for a variety of special tasks other than those for which they were originally trained.

It was, perhaps, a natural thing to do, and it might have been acceptable if the Special Forces soldiers, whose average age was about thirty, were used only for really special operations. However, that was not the case, and any general who had a special "pet" project inevitably demanded a complement of Special Forces to carry it out. Such projects were invariably operations that the Special Forces were not really trained for, but their abilities, experience, and skill usually carried them through to success.

This misuse of the Special Forces has perhaps been the cause of the media's considerable misunderstanding concerning their true role, and subsequently the misunderstanding was transmitted to the general public.

In order to maintain secrecy, the Army deliberately defined the role of the Special Forces in an obscure way. The Army Field Manual that applies to them states that the Special Forces will "assume any responsibility and carry out any mission assigned by the Army." It is this definition that is most often quoted by the media; it is also used by military men, who know better, for the purpose of obtaining Special Forces soldiers for their own pet projects.

Although the Special Forces commanders object to the misuse of their forces for special missions, they would not like to see the practice stopped entirely, as some of the missions afford an interesting change from routine and provide not only excitement but an opportunity for the men to practice some of the skills they teach.

At the time of their inception in 1952, the primary concern of the Special Forces was to establish themselves to conduct guerrilla-warfare operations in European nations that were being threatened with invasion by the Soviet Union.

In 1949, the United States government, under the leadership of President Truman, became acutely alarmed when they discovered that the Soviet Union was making plans to take over Europe by force (a fact that was first proved by the British, West German, French, and American intelligence organizations and later admitted by the Soviets). With confirmation of the Soviets' intentions, President Truman immediately ordered the strengthening of our defense capability, which had been greatly depleted since the end of World War II.

When President Eisenhower was elected in 1952, he dramatically accelerated the buildup of American forces and also the nation's nuclear-missile capability. This became known as the "Massive Retaliation Capability," intended solely to prevent the takeover of Europe by the Communist forces. During 1953, amid the growing threat of a Soviet invasion, Eisenhower authorized the deployment of the 10th Special Forces in Europe and further increased the pace of the deployment of nuclear missiles and armed forces.

When the Soviets realized that the United States and its North Atlantic Treaty Organization allies (NATO) had built up both their conventional forces and nuclear arsenals to such an extent that any attempt to take Europe by force could prove disastrous, they changed their tactics. They decided that a quick victory was not to be had in Europe and that they could ultimately achieve their stated goal of world domination by careful long-term planning and covert operations.

In a brilliant countermaneuver to the Massive Retaliation concept, the Soviet Communists devised their program of "wars of liberation," featuring subversion, insurgency, and unconventional-warfare operations. As they infiltrated almost every country imaginable in their attempts to establish themselves, they still maintained the appearance that they intended to take Europe with their conventional armies.

By maintaining the threat of an all-out war in Europe, they effectively deceived the United States and the member nations of NATO. This earned them valuable time in which to establish their clandestine influence operations in all parts of the world, with little or no opposition from the United States and its allies.

Not all the members of NATO were deceived, but, unfortunately, they were in the minority. It took them considerable time to convince their colleagues that Massive Retaliation by itself would not stop the spread of Communist influence, subterfuge, and conquest.

Within the United States military, a small group of men fought desperately to establish a means to counter the global flanking maneuver of the Communists' regime. It was a hard fight, as the majority of high-ranking government officials, military leaders, and advisers accused them of scare mongering. It was not until various international intelligence networks started to confirm what they were saying that they began to gather more support, and they eventually received authorization to pursue the development of effective countermeasures.

Authorization, however, did not mean that establishing special forces groups would be easy; there were enough high-ranking officers in supply, and support commands who not only objected to the idea of special forces but who were in a position to make life difficult for those trying to build the new group by being slow to cooperate. But the adversity was eventually overcome, and tribute must be paid to those very determined men, for it is because of them that the Army Special Forces exists today.

In fairness to the military leaders of the time, it must be pointed out that they agreed that something had to be done about the rapidly spreading Communist insurgency movement. However, the senior establishment of *all* the United States Armed Forces did not like the formation of elite groups within their ranks; They genuinely believed that the problem would be handled by conventional military units (although not as severe, that attitude is, unfortunately, still quite prevalent among some senior military leaders and officials of the Department of Defense).

It would appear that perhaps the only reason the senior members of the military agreed to permit the formation of the Special Forces and Special Operations groups within their ranks was that the CIA and the State Department, and to a lesser degree the FBI, were actively seeking responsibility for all counterinsurgency and counterguerrilla operations. Regardless of their objections to elite groups, the military was not prepared to concede total control of such operations to the nonmilitary groups.

However, the reluctance of our military leaders to foster elite groups must be understood, since it was, for the most part, based on genuine concern. They believed that to take all the best men and place them in elite groups was foolish, as that would lower the standards of the remainder of the armed forces. Good men, they felt, should be distributed throughout the armed forces, where their abilities and qualities would serve to improve the standards of the *entire* force.

Unfortunately, that line of reasoning does not appear to be quite right, as a study of volunteers for elite fighting units—and in particular the men who volunteered for one of the most disciplined of World War II elite units, the Darby Ranger battalions—clearly shows that almost all the enlisted personnel, and most of the officers, were near renegades from conventional military organizations.

They were not, however, attempting to escape from military discipline when they volunteered for the Rangers, because almost all of them knew that discipline was infinitely more strict in the elite Ranger battalions. Neither were they outcasts from society, thugs, rogues, convicts, or other reprobates—they were simply individuals with a high sense of daring and a fierce will to be warriors. The United States, their free nation, was at war with forces that were apparently trying to deprive them of their freedom, and the Ranger volunteers were men who desperately wanted to have an active part in the actual fighting.

Documented psychological studies to determine the reasons why such men have an apparent suicidal desire to be in the front line would fill a large room, but all that really matters—particularly when a nation desperately needs valiant warriors—is that there are men who want to do it. Every man who volunteered to join Darby's battalions during World War II was searching either for something different in military life, or the opportunity to get into battle as soon as possible. For whatever reason, it appears that the volunteers finally fulfilled their quest in the ranks of the Rangers. In doing so, they also served their nation in an exemplary manner, by undertaking missions that much larger conventional units could not have completed without suffering incredible casualties.

Fortunately for the United States, today's volunteers for the Special Forces are not much different from the men who made up the Ranger battalions and other elite fighting groups of World War II.

Because elite groups are invariably given a lot of publicity and generally attract considerable attention, there is a tendency for the more traditional military units to feel somewhat inferior and to believe that they are nothing more than cannon fodder. This obviously does nothing to help morale, which, in a peacetime army, is one of the most difficult things to achieve and sustain. Opponents of the formation of elite units have a valid argument in this respect, as the existence of such groups does have a slightly demoralizing effect on the majority of the traditional units.

However, it has been shown that sound judgment and good leadership skills, with an emphasis on the welfare and well-being of all soldiers by their appointed leaders, from noncommissioned officers to generals, will produce a very high standard of morale and efficiency in any conventional military organization.

It has also been shown, and many commanders of conventional military units will attest to it, that highly intense and dedicated individual warriors within a conventional unit can have a disruptive effect. They unavoidably expose the minor deficiencies of their fellow soldiers, and that tends to produce unnecessary inferiority complexes, which ultimately have a detrimental effect on the entire unit.

During extended periods of peace, it is almost impossible to maintain full-size conventional units at a high state of readiness, whereas the smaller elite groups tend to thrive on the requirement to be constantly alert. Invariably, during such periods of peace, extremely urgent situations that demand a rapid military response arise. Experience has shown that such situations are best handled by a force that is not only willing but is rapidly deployable, has the required training and experienced personnel, and has the necessary specialist equipment immediately available.

The incident concerning the tiny island of Grenada

is a first-class example, and it was handled quickly and efficiently by a coordinated effort of most of the United States elite fighting forces: Marines, Rangers, SEALs, and Air Commandos, in conjunction with supporting elements of the Navy, the Air Force, and the Army's 82nd Airborne. (Contrary to popular belief, the Army Special Forces were used in an extremely limited and specialized role. Almost all the credit for the success of the operation must go to other elite forces.)

The idea that elite groups can be formed and brought up to peak efficiency at short notice, as has been the policy in the past, is entirely wrong. History has conclusively proved that philosophy to be a fallacy.

Regardless of all the arguments against elite military groups, the object of war, in the thinking of almost every so-called civilized and uncivilized nation, is to defeat the opponent with the least possible casualty count. All military records concerning the history of this earth clearly show that elite fighting forces have been one of the most efficient means of achieving that end. It is therefore reasonably safe to assume that the formation and maintenance of elite fighting groups as adjuncts to a nation's primary defense force is to the benefit of the conventional military establishment and the nation itself.

When both the Soviet Union and the Communist Chinese started their global campaign of insurgency and insurrection, in their "wars of liberation," the Special Forces were compelled to expand their area of operations outside Europe. This expansion was not just a desire on the part of the Special Forces to grow into a large organization, nor was it caused by the United States government attempting to exert its influence over other nations. It occurred in response to requests for assistance from numerous nations that wished to remain free from Communist domination.

During the past twenty years, the kaleidoscope of changing social, political, economic, and territorial doctrines has revealed a situation where even the most nonmilitary-minded can see that the traditional use of conventional armies is either utterly impotent or an unnecessary use of force, or both.

The failure of the massive armies of the Union of Soviet and Socialist Republic in Afghanistan, against scrawny, ragged, mountain tribesmen, has become obvious to people all over the world and is a classic example of the impotence of a large, highly trained, well-equipped conventional army. By the same token, and regrettably for ourselves, the failure of the attempts of our own mighty forces to keep the Republic of Vietnam free from Communist rule is another example.

In both cases, guerrilla warfare was, and still is, the problem, and it is somewhat ironic to see the Soviet Army struggling badly against the guerrillas of Afghanistan, as the Soviets have always claimed to be both the originators and the masters of guerrilla warfare. Although we lost the war in Vietnam, because of self-imposed political restraints relating to our foreign policy and because of a self-imposed withdrawal, we did not lose the guerrilla war.

The first Special Forces soldiers arrived in Vietnam in 1957 and spent almost a year assisting with the formation and training of a Vietnamese Special Forces unit. In May 1960, thirty Special Forces soldiers were sent to establish a training program for the Vietnamese Army, and from that point on, Special Forces involvement increased. By the end of 1971, all major elements of the Special Forces, as well as our conventional units, had been withdrawn from the country, and the people of South Vietnam were left to defend themselves. They were defeated by the Vietcong guerrilla forces and the regular army of North Vietnam, both of which were still entirely supported and equipped by Communist China and the Soviet Union.

During eleven continuous years of involvement in Vietnam, the Special Forces were winning. Not because they say so, but because leaders of the Vietcong and North Vietnamese armies have since openly admitted that they were losing ground to the Special Forces' organized resistance. Any Special Forces veteran who spent enough time in Vietnam will admit that the war could have been won, but will also admit that it would have taken perhaps another ten or fifteen years to do it.

To the average citizen, to the members of our government, and to our military leaders, that is a frightening length of time for a war to continue. Unfortunately, most people think in terms of massive conventional wars, which normally last only a few years, and for that kind of war even a few years is too long. However, regardless of how horrifying the idea might be, that sort of thinking simply cannot be applied to unconventional and guerrilla warfare, and in particular to counterguerrilla warfare, which is what the Vietnam war was.

Any nation that becomes involved in a future guerrilla war must accept the fact that the fight will be very long and arduous, and if it is a counterguerrilla war it will perhaps be even longer. There will be no quick victory and no easy solution, for many reasons, one of which is the fact that it appears that almost all future wars will be fought over ideological differences and not simple territorial violations, as they have been in the past.

Examples of this kind of war can presently be found almost everywhere in the world; a few are as follows: Lebanon in the Middle East; Vietnam/Cambodia/Thailand in Southeast Asia; El Salvador/Nicaragua/Honduras in South America; Chad/Angola/Somalia in Africa; Northern Ireland in Europe.

The thought of the United States getting involved in a war of this nature is not a pleasant one, but if we are to assist our faithful allies to maintain what freedom they have, and if we are to help defend other nations that beg for our assistance to remain free, we will inevitably become involved. By acting quickly, as in the case of Grenada, we might be able to avert potentially difficult and protracted engagements, but we will not always be so lucky.

For the freedom of other nations and our own national security, and in order to minimize the strain on the resources of the United States, we must utilize the dedicated warriors of the Special Forces in the role for which they have been trained—that of teaching the skills of unconventional warfare.

The dictionary definition of *terrorism* states that it is the "use of terror for the purpose of coercion," but the more accepted definition is "indiscriminate acts of violence perpetrated against innocent people by individuals or groups seeking to further their own cause." The latter description best describes the acts of international terrorism that started to increase in the mid-1970s. Apart from the British SAS (which had foreseen the problem and had trained extensively to deal with it), and a special unit of the Israeli Army, no other military organization existed among the nations of the free world, or the Soviet bloc nations, that had a first-class specialist counterterrorist capability.

The West Germans were quick to follow the British; they established, with the help of the SAS, their GSG-9 (*Grenzschutzgruppe-9*, which literally translated means *Frontier-defense Group 9*). In October 1977, when the GSG-9 completed their successful antiterrorist action against the hijackers of a West German airliner at Mogadishu airport, Somalia, they were accompanied by two experienced members of the British SAS. The commanders of the GSG-9 had requested not only their help but also the use of some of their specialized equipment, and when the operation was completed they unintentionally embarrassed the SAS by openly thanking them for their assistance.

At that time, the Department of the Army, under the direction of the Joint Chiefs of Staff, had already initiated a program to develop our own specialist counterterrorist group. The group was called the 1st Special Forces Operational Detachment-Delta, SFOD-Delta, now more commonly called the Delta Force. When the Mogadishu incident occurred, Delta Force was only in the planning stage, and it had been agreed by everyone that it was to be organized almost entirely along the lines of the British SAS. Furthermore, it was being established by Special Forces officers who had been trained extensively by the SAS, but it did not come under the control of the Special Forces Command; instead it answered directly to the Chiefs of Staff of the Army.

As a result of the Mogadishu episode, pressure was applied to rapidly produce the Delta Force. However, the Special Forces officer assigned to form Delta had originally said it would take two years to prepare the unit for operation, and he flatly refused to accelerate the program. During consultations with the commanders of the SAS, he had been strongly advised not to take a day less than eighteen months—two years, if possible. It was sound advice, and the Joint Chiefs of Staff accepted the Special Forces officer's suggestion.

However, the idea that the United States would be without an effective counterterrorist organization for almost two years did not sit well with the Special Forces. As a result, within the 5th Special Forces Group at Fort Bragg, a counterterrorist unit called the Blue Lights was rapidly formed and trained. This unit effectively bridged the gap until the infant Delta Force got its feet squarely on the ground.

Today, in 1985, the United States Army Special Forces groups in active service are as follows:

The 5th and 7th Special Forces Groups are based at Fort Bragg, North Carolina.

The 10th Special Forces Group is based at Fort Devens, Massachusetts.

The 1st Special Forces Group, recently reactivated, is based at Fort Lewis, Washington.

The 3rd Battalion of the 7th Special Forces Group is stationed in Panama.

The 1st Battalion of the 10th Special Forces Group is stationed in West Germany.

The 1st Battalion of the 1st Special Forces Group is stationed in Okinawa.

Special Forces in reserve are: 11th and 12th Special Forces (U.S. Army Reserve), and 19th and 20th Special Forces (U.S. Army National Guard).

8
BATTLEFIELD LOG:
War Zone C, Vietnam—December, 1966

When the U-2 pilot realized that his aircraft was in trouble, he quickly decided to bail out. As he carried out the mandatory security procedures for his highly sophisticated reconnaissance aircraft, he briefly remembered an incident that had occurred some six years earlier over the Soviet Union.

In that incident, a U-2 reconnaissance aircraft—very similar to the one he was now about to bail out of in mid-air—had been knocked out of the sky by a Soviet Surface-to-Air Missile (SAM). The pilot of that aircraft was Francis Gary Powers, and when he bailed out over Sverdlovsk, some seven hundred miles east of Moscow, he was taken prisoner and placed on trial as a spy.

In addition to the fact that it was an international incident that obviously embarrassed the United States, the aircraft was not totally destroyed and fell into the hands of the Soviets. The information which that gleaned from the wreckage of the craft, and that which they forcibly extracted from Powers, was highly classified and was to the detriment of our national security.

Knowing that he was now faced with a similar situation over Southeast Asia, the Air Force pilot made every attempt to ensure that he operated the required security functions. Satisfied that he had done all he could, the pilot bailed out safely and watched his aircraft disappear into dense jungle near the Cambodian border.

As he was leaving his stricken craft, the Air Force rescue teams and the Air Commando pilots and crews were already scrambling for their search-and-rescue helicopters and aircraft. Within a very short time the downed pilot was located and picked up, just as enemy ground forces were getting close to him. Extensive searching by reconnaissance aircraft failed to locate the wreckage of the U-2, despite the fact that the Air Force, based on information received from the pilot of the downed craft, was certain that they knew the general area into which the aircraft had plummeted.

When they finally realized that they would not be able to locate the aircraft wreckage from the air, the Air Force informed General William Westmoreland, Commander in Chief, Southeast Asia, that they required assistance. They also informed him that, unfortunately, one item in the aircraft would still be intact—a "black box"—and they definitely did not wish to suffer the embarrassment of its falling into enemy hands. General Westmoreland contacted Colonel Francis Kelly, Commanding Officer of the 5th Special Forces Group, and requested a ground-search team of Special Forces soldiers.

When Colonel Kelly was given the details of the crash, he realized immediately why General Westmoreland had requested the Special Forces to handle the affair. The U-2 had gone down in an area known as War Zone C, and the particular sector where the crash had occurred was entirely in the hands of the North Vietnamese Communists.

The jungle in War Zone C was not as bad as that in other parts of Vietnam, Laos, and Cambodia. For the most part, the trees were between twenty and fifty feet high and formed a double upper canopy that restricted visibility in the jungle only to about one hundred feet. There were considerably more open spaces and clearings in this region, most of which were covered with ten-foot-high elephant grass, and there was the inevitable assortment of tortuous bamboo thickets scattered throughout the area.

The search-and-rescue operation was assigned to the men of A Company, 5th Special Forces Group, whose regional headquarters were at Bein Hoa, some thirty miles north of Saigon.

The commander of A Company, Lieutenant Colonel Thomas Huddleston, allocated the mission to his rapid-deploy group, the Third Mobile Strike Force, more commonly known as a "Mike Force." In command of the Third Mike Force was Captain James "Bo" Gritz, a quick-thinking, energetic, responsible leader who was delighted to be assigned the mission. His total Mike Force strength was approximately 600 men, comprised of three companies of about 150 men, three reconnaissance platoons of 35 men, and one 12-man command team called an A Team.

Apart from the men of the A Team and the leaders of the reconnaissance teams, who were all U.S. Army Special Forces, all remaining personnel were Special Forces–trained Vietnamese Civilian Irregular Defense Group (CIDG) and regular Vietnamese Army personnel. The majority of the Vietnamese in the Mike Force were fierce Nung tribesmen from the North Vietnam/China border region who were known for their intense loyalty to the American Special Forces.

Captain Gritz had no sooner received word of the mission than a group of Air Force officers arrived at Bein Hoa with maps of the crash area and photographs of a typical U-2. They explained to the Special Forces men how to locate and extract the secret black box, assuming that they were successful in locating the aircraft; they also explained how several other items should be destroyed if they were still intact.

The Special Forces personnel were all very experienced jungle operators, and they became quite alarmed when the Air Force revealed the size and location of the triangular search area. They were further surprised when the Air Force officers admitted that the chosen search area was actually only their best guess, based solely on the recovery point of the downed pilot and the direction in which the aircraft had been heading when he had been forced to bail out.

Because the search area was in the middle of a Vietcong haven, Captain Gritz decided to employ a company-sized force of 150 Nungs, plus a 35-man reconnaissance platoon and his own Special Forces A Team; the remainder of his Mike Force were to go on standby to act as a relief force, if necessary. The 197-man team he had chosen gave him a highly mobile force with multiple heavy machine guns, grenade launchers, ample automatic-rifle men, radio technicians, medics, snipers, and various other specialized personnel and weapons. The Air Force gave their support by assigning their famous Air Commando AC-47 Spooky gunships, A-1 Skyraider fighter bombers, called "flying dump trucks" because of the tonnage of bombs, rockets, and ammunition they could carry, and a variety of other specialized aircraft.

As a result, the team was not only a well-armed, highly mobile ground fighting force, it also had the size, experience, and necessary air support to handle almost any threat that either the Vietcong or even the regular

North Vietnamese Army could throw against it in War Zone C.

A fleet of helicopters infiltrated the strike force into the search area, and no attempt was made to conceal the fact that a large force was being deployed. The search commenced at the apex of the triangular area designated by the Air Force and progressed slowly into the depths of the enemy-held territory. Gritz and his men discovered that the entire area was a maze of trails and tunnels through the jungle, and it became obvious by the end of the first day that these trails were well used by small enemy-supply columns, couriers, and bands of raiders. It was also obvious, because of the almost complete lack of security precautions on the part of the enemy using the trails, that the enemy felt the entire area was safe from attack.

The first incident that brought this fact to light occurred not more than an hour after the strike force had landed in the jungle. The entire team was moving along a trail in a westerly direction when the scouts of the reconnaissance platoon ambushed a well-armed party of six Vietcong who were approaching from the opposite direction. The enemy soldiers were chatting noisily to one another and were paying almost no attention to what was going on around them. The reconnaissance platoon wiped out the entire group in a short firefight when the enemy tried to flee after they discovered they had walked into an ambush.

For three days the strike force worked their way back and forth across the appointed area in their search for the crashed U-2. They were constantly running into small bands of Vietcong, who always appeared to be completely surprised, and most of the firefights never lasted more than a few minutes.

One of the more amusing aspects of the operation was the fact that the entire area was saturated with propaganda leaflets that were continually being dropped by the PSYOPS Units of the Air Commando. This caused one seasoned Special Forces officer to comment that he thought it was quite a magnanimous gesture on the part of the United States government to supply the Vietcong with toilet paper (although never officially documented, most of the Special Forces, CIA, and other military personnel who operated in Vietnam confirm that propaganda leaflets were used extensively by the enemy and the civilian population for that very purpose).

Early in the afternoon of the third day, the strike force was deep in the dense jungles of the enemy-held territory when one of Nungs in the reconnaissance platoon stopped and started to sniff the air. He smelled something that was not usually associated with the jungle, and shortly afterward the remaining members of his group, including the Special Forces noncommissioned officers, picked up the same smell. Thirty minutes later, the patrol found the wrecked U-2, and shortly afterward Captain Gritz and the remainder of the strike force arrived at the wreckage.

The best guess of the Air Force had turned out to be accurate, but the elation of the strike force did not last long, for they soon discovered that there was no black box! Careful examination of the wreckage revealed that the enemy had been there and had removed the box. They obviously knew its importance.

Captain Gritz decided not to give up hope. He reasoned that if the enemy had taken the trouble to remove the box, there was a strong possibility that most of the Vietcong in the entire War Zone would know of its existence; with that, he concluded that what they needed was a few Vietcong prisoners. When he was certain that nothing else on the wrecked U-2 was of use to the enemy, he informed his men of his intentions and instructed them to actively seek out the enemy and capture as many of them as possible for some rapid field interrogation.

Bo Gritz and every member of the strike force were well aware that attempting to capture Vietcong prisoners was extremely dangerous and difficult. Wounded Vietcong normally put up such fierce resistance that they were unapproachable and had to be shot from a distance. Attempts to take them prisoner almost always resulted in severe casualties being suffered by the attacking force.

The strike force moved away from the wreckage and started to hunt for more-familiar prey than the black box. They did not have to look far before they found it, but unfortunately they failed to keep any of the enemy alive long enough to question them. Several more attempts ended up the same way, and, as expected, the strike force was starting to incur casualties in their attempts to wound rather than kill the enemy. Eventually, one of the Special Forces snipers managed to lightly wound a Vietcong and then destroy his weapon with some superb shooting. As the Vietcong tried to get away into the jungle, a group of Nungs raced after him and managed to subdue him after a fierce struggle.

By the time the Nungs eventually dragged the Vietcong out of the jungle and back to Captain Gritz, he had suffered a few more injuries—he did not allow himself to be captured easily. The medics immediately started to treat the man's wounds, despite his continued resistance, and the interrogation began.

Slowly but surely the Nung interrogators persuaded the Vietcong prisoner to reveal that he knew of the existence of the black box. Eventually, he revealed that it was still within the War Zone and that it had been removed only a short time before the strike force had reached the wreckage. One final interrogation session produced the required information—the box was being held in a Vietcong camp that held a sizable enemy force and was due to be collected within a few days by couriers from the north.

After considerable persuasion, the wounded Vietcong agreed to lead the strike force to the camp where the box was being held; in return, he was promised that he would be taken to the relative safety of a prisoner-of-war camp.

When they neared the Vietcong base camp, the reconnaissance platoon went forward to carefully survey the area. On their return, they reported what they had discovered to Captain Gritz, who decided that he would make no attempt to surround the camp and start a protracted fight. Instead, he would lead the entire force straight into the middle of the camp and force the enemy to take cover while he and his men searched for the box.

A few men were assigned to guard the prisoner and the wounded strike-force members while the rest of the force went toward the base camp. They reached the edge of the enemy stronghold without being discovered. Then, on a signal from Gritz, the entire force charged into the camp with rifles and machine guns blazing. The enemy were taken completely by surprise and fled into the jungle and into numerous tunnels around the camp. Within moments, the only people in the camp were the Special Forces soldiers, who quickly started to search the numerous small huts.

It took very little time to find the elusive black box, and Gritz immediately ordered his force to retreat into the jungle. As they left the camp they hurled grenades into the buildings and destroyed everything in sight. Having collected their wounded soldiers and the Vietcong prisoner, they started a hasty retreat toward their insertion point.

The Vietcong who had fled the base camp regrouped and set out after the strike force. Messages were sent to all other Vietcong camps in the area informing them of the situation and the direction in which the Mike Force had departed. The enemy were now intent on destroying the force and recapturing the black box.

Gritz knew that once he attacked the camp, every Vietcong in the entire War Zone would be utilized to search for them and that he would have to fight his way out. The Mike Force was deep in the jungle and it would take several days of fast moving and fighting to get to a clearing that was large enough for the entire force to be airlifted out. However, when a tiny clearing was located, Gritz decided to seize the opportunity to get the black box out of the jungle along with his wounded men and the Vietcong prisoner.

On December 25, 1966, with the Air Commando A-1s providing tight overhead cover, the rescue helicopters dropped their rescue lines down through the trees and snatched the black box, the prisoner, and the wounded strike-force members out of the jungle. As soon as they had left, Captain Gritz and the remainder of the strike force set off into the jungle again.

For the next two days the strike force fought a running battle with a fanatical enemy who were enraged that their territory had been penetrated and that they had lost their precious spoil from the crashed U-2. The Air Commando answered every call for assistance from the strike force and were continually bombing and strafing through the jungle canopy at an enemy they could not see.

Finally, the strike force reached a clear area, and a fleet of helicopters and supporting A-1s arrived and lifted them to safety.

Captain James Gritz and the men of the Third Mobile Strike Force had ventured into territory that had never been penetrated by either South Vietnamese or American forces. They had harassed the Vietcong in their own backyard and had acutely embarrassed them by recovering the black box. Perhaps the most significant fact was that the majority of the men in the Third Mobile Strike Force were native to Vietnam, and they clearly demonstrated the level of professionalism that could be achieved by the dedication, leadership, teaching, and training skills of the U.S. Army Special Forces.

9

SPECIAL FORCES TRAINING

Before a member of the United States Army—either commissioned or enlisted—can apply to join the Special Forces, he must first be recommended by his commanding officer. A volunteer will not be recommended by his commanding officer if he does not have certain specified qualifications; however, there are some requirements, other than those which are physical, that can be waived by the Commandant of the Army Institute for Military Assistance. Each applicant must presently have a "Secret" level security clearance, must be airborne-qualified, must speak a second language (or have the interest and the ability to learn at least one more language), must meet the required physical-fitness standards, and must have completed the Combat Water Survival Test (CWST).

The Combat Water Survival Test has three basic parts, the first of which is the fifteen-meter swim. The applicant must wear a soft cap, fatigues, boots, pistol belt, first-aid pouch, two canteens filled with water, two ammunition pouches, harness, and a rifle. He must step backward into the water, then surface, turn around, and swim a minimum of fifteen meters without losing his equipment.

The second part of the test is called "equipment removal." Wearing the same equipment as for the fifteen-meter swim, the applicant must jump into a pool where the water depth is at least over his head, surface and compose himself, then submerge, drop the rifle and remove all his equipment while submerged, then surface again and swim to safety without showing any sign of panic.

The final part of the test is the three-meter drop. The applicant, equipped as for the previous parts of the test, is blindfolded and must step off a three-meter-high platform and fall into the water. He must surface, compose himself, then remove the blindfold only, and swim to safety.

Although this test might seem quite simple to complete, it is not. Many a proficient swimmer has failed it because his ability to swim was completely negated by the equipment, by the reduced temperature of the water in which the test is conducted, or by panic that results from the discovery that clothing and equipment have a marked tendency to cause sinking and an extreme lack of mobility.

Officer volunteers must be from the combat arms of the Army, apart from certain other prerequisites called for in Army regulations, they must also have the following: a high ability and efficiency grade; a minimum of one year combat-arms troop duty experience; an actual or anticipated requirement or assignment that necessitates a working knowledge of unconventional warfare and Special Forces operational techniques; at least one year to serve in the Army after completion of Special Forces training.

Enlisted volunteers, apart from basic prerequisites covered by Army regulations, are required to satisfy the following criteria: consistent high grades and achievements in their Military Occupational Specialties; a high-school diploma or the equivalent academic qualifications; a minimum of fourteen months to serve after completion of Special Forces training.

Once all the initial requirements have been satisfied, officer and enlisted candidates must complete the Special Forces Qualification Course—more commonly called the Q Course. During the course, candidates are constantly tested and evaluated; should they fail to meet the required standards, at any stage in the course, they will be discharged and returned to their original units.

In the past, the qualification course was just sixteen weeks in duration, and, upon graduating, a soldier simply added another successfully completed course to his list of qualifications. However, that has recently been changed, and apart from the fact that the courses have been extended considerably—most to twenty-six weeks—graduation now results in the achievement of a new Military Occupational Specialty (MOS), which in simple terms means a designated trade or profession for which there is an appropriate pay scale, etc. This change was brought about for several reasons, both financial and administrative, but perhaps the primary reason was that a better-qualified Special Forces soldier would be produced to meet the demands of modern unconventional warfare.

The new course is divided into five specialist sections, disciplines, or Military Occupational Specialties; four of them are assigned specifically for enlisted personnel and one is for officers.

The five disciplines are as follows: Special Forces Medical Sergeant; Special Forces Weapons Sergeant; Special Forces Engineer Sergeant; Special Forces Communication Sergeant; and Special Forces Detachment Officer.

Special Forces Medical Sergeant

This is the longest course of the specialist disciplines; it takes forty-four weeks to complete. The majority of the course is taught in Army hospitals and medical centers with extensive practical exposure. Included in the course are combat medicine, emergency surgical procedures, and partial traumatic amputation without hospital facilities or the supervision of a surgeon. Also included in the Medical Sergeants training is an extensive course in veterinary medicine, since livestock management often plays a vital part in the life of remote native villages.

Special Forces Weapons Sergeant

This specialist discipline course is twenty-six weeks long and involves training in all aspects of light- and heavy-weapon employment, maintenance, and operation. Instruction and field training are given with all U.S., NATO, and Warsaw Pact military weapons, both current and obsolete, and a wide range of civilian weapons. It also covers a variety of specialist weapons from China and various other arms-manufacturing nations.

Special Forces Engineer Sergeant

This twenty-six-week course includes operation of every known and available type of commercial- and military-manufactured explosive; manufacture and use of "home-made" explosives; special demolitions and the fabrication of unusual explosive devices. The course also includes basic civil-engineering instruction, construction equipment and tools, and practical modern construction techniques applicable to Special Forces assignments. One segment of the course deals specifically with expedient construction techniques in remote and isolated areas where modern tools and equipment are not available.

Special Forces Communication Sergeant

This course is twenty-six weeks long and includes extended-range conventional-warfare communications; Special Forces communications requirements including the use of codes and special operating procedures; use, care, and maintenance of the various types of specialized communications available to the Special Forces only; extensive training in the use of the international Morse code to a high level of proficiency.

Special Forces Detachment Officer

This twenty-six-week course is designed to train and educate detachment commanders. It covers all aspects of command and control of Special Forces teams, their use and employment, in all areas of the world. The course also includes extensive training in intelligence operations, cultural relations, civic affairs, logistics, and operational doctrines and procedures.

Although the Q Course is broken down into these five separate disciplines, a considerable amount of the subject material covered in each course is common to all five courses. This common material could be classed as Special Forces general procedures and field-operating techniques, and it includes training in the following subjects: Briefings and Orientations; Survival; Special Airborne Training Operations; Patrolling; Intelligence; Map Reading and Land Navigation; Unconventional Warfare; General Subjects.

Briefings and Orientations

This is basically the first course, as it includes an introduction to the Special Forces, their history and present organizational structure. Also included in this is a short course on emergency medical treatment, or first aid.

Survival

This course segment covers the following: location of natural field shelters and construction of field shelters; direction finding in the field without compass or other navigational aids; ropes and knot tying; construction of rope bridges; construction of rafts and other rudimentary vessels for water transportation; poisonous snakes; signaling techniques; fire building and cooking devices; procurement of food and water; poisonous and edible plants; preparation of fish and game; survival planning and survival kits; physiological and psychological aspects of extended periods of survival in hostile environments.

Special Airborne Training and Operations

This course covers all the techniques utilized by the Special Forces for parachuting into enemy-held territory, such as rigging equipment and weapons in preparation for an air drop, and includes operating from helicopters.

Patrolling

This course covers advanced day- and night-patrolling techniques; reconnaissance patrols; ambush patrols; raiding techniques; operating bases for patrols; patrol planning; recording and reporting intelligence information; operation orders and warning orders.

Intelligence

This course introduces candidates to field intelligence operations; Special Forces intelligence requirements: identification systems; interrogation processes; operational photography and field equipment; target analysis and interdiction operations; electronic warfare in Special Forces operations; escape and evasion; tactical deception; clandestine operations and intelligence briefings.

Map Reading and Land Navigation

This course covers map reading and map symbols, both United States and foreign; military grid-reference system; elevation and relief; direction and azimuths; scales and distance measuring; advanced compass and map orientation; intersection and resection; terrain association; practical land navigation exercises and techniques.

Unconventional Warfare

This course covers the fundamentals of unconventional warfare; organization and development of resistance forces; underground operations; establishment of operation areas and an underground command structure; training of resistance forces; general guerrilla-warfare operations; urban area guerrilla-warfare operations; demobilization; logistics in unconventional warfare; subversion and sabotage operations; psychological operations in support of unconventional warfare; civil affairs in support of unconventional warfare; maritime operations and United States Air Force and Air Commando support of unconventional-warfare operations.

General Subjects

This course covers elementary field radio communications and operations; responsibilities of individual Special Forces soldiers; snipers and their use; close air-support operations and forward air control; demolition operations; interpretation of aerial reconnaissance photography; mission planning and preparation; terrorism and counterterrorism; infiltration and exfiltration planning; foreign internal defense; intercultural communications; U.S. security-assistance programs and Mobile Training Team operations.

At the end of each Q Course there are various written and practical tests, but the final examination is an operational field exercise called "Robin Sage."

This exercise is conducted in an unconventional-warfare scenario, and the object is for the student to demonstrate his complete understanding of everything he has learned during the Q Course. Failure to perform well on Robin Sage will result in a student's being returned to his original unit. However, failure at this stage is very rare, as most candidates who are unsuitable are discovered long before this stage of the course. Passing the course simply qualifies a soldier to become a member of a Special Forces A Detachment, or field team, but it is really only the beginning.

Graduates from the Q Course who do not already speak a second language must now learn one, and there are extensive courses in various other specialist operations that are peculiar to Special Forces requirements and are of a classified nature. Further advanced courses are as follows: Civil Affairs; Civil-Military Operations; Psychological Operations; Base Communications Establishment; Underwater Operations; Diving Supervisor; Medical Diving Technician; Submarine Operations; Free-fall Parachuting; Free-fall Jumpmaster; High Altitude Parachuting; Intelligence Operations.

Apart from these courses there are attachments and assignments to other services in the United States Armed Forces and to the armed forces of various NATO countries for the purpose of learning other specialist skills for use in unconventional warfare.

In conclusion, it is safe to say that the Special Forces soldier is almost always training or being retrained in order to prepare him as much as possible for demands that might be placed on him in the fulfillment of his duties.

10

BATTLEFIELD LOG:
Ben Het, Vietnam—February 19, 1968

The air cover over the jungle canopy was filled with the dull *whapping* sound of eight UH-1 Huey helicopters as they crossed over the border of South Vietnam into Laos.

As the reference markers that designated the border disappeared beneath the lead helicopter, the pilot pressed the radio transmitter switch on his control stick and called out a brief control word.

Almost one hundred miles to the northeast, the code word was received and acknowledged by the Special Operations Group command and control center at Marble Mountain, Da Nang.

The code word was the signal to the command center that the helicopter formation had just crossed the border near Ben Het, in the province of Kontum, and that their mission had now officially started. The controller who had received the message in the command center moved over to a large area map showing Vietnam, Laos, and Cambodia, and placed in the southeastern corner of Laos a small marker flag carrying the words *Shining Brass* and a series of numbers.

* * *

"Shining Brass" was the code name given to a program of cross-border operations into Laos. These operations were intended to interrupt the steady flow of regular North Vietnamese Army troops, munitions, and supplies that were being routed down through Laos and Cambodia into South Vietnam. The North Vietnamese had been forced to use these routes, contrary to the will of both the Cambodian and the Laotian people, as combined South Vietnamese and American forces had effectively choked off the routes across the border in the demilitarized zone between North and South Vietnam.

Laos, at that time, was also having problems with Communist insurgents and guerrillas, and all penetration missions from South Vietnam required the approval of the American ambassador to that nation. It appears that he then obtained approval for the raids from the Laotian premier, Souvanna Phouma, and the non-Communist element of the Laotian government. Further approval was also required from the Central Intelligence Agency station chief in the Laotian capital of Vientiane, and also from the Chiefs of Staff in the Pentagon.

With such a procedure there was obviously a tremendous risk of a breach of security—more commonly called a "leak"—and indeed many of the Special Forces teams who carried out the raids became involved in situations where the enemy really did appear to be waiting for them.

However, once approval for a penetration mission was finally granted, the normal procedure was to send in a reconnaissance team—which was not permitted to penetrate more than twenty kilometers into Laos—and they would feed back target information for air strikes or whatever action was considered necessary.

On the morning of February 19, 1968—when the Shining Brass flag appeared on the map in the tactical-

operations room of the Special Operations Group
headquarters—various Army, Air Force, Navy, and Marine personnel staff members opened the log books and
signal pads that lay by their communications equipment, recorded the time of the border crossing, and
then settled down to wait in nervous anticipation.

These mixed military personnel were the critical
operations coordinators for the cross-border operations,
and the flag that the controller had placed on the map
was the signal that the reconnaissance team had crossed
the Laotian border. From that moment on, the joint
services coordinators could be called upon to organize a
variety of support operations, such as air strikes, troop
reinforcements, and medical evacuations or rescue missions for the pilots and crews of helicopters or strike
aircraft that might get shot down. The coordinators,
almost without exception, always became a little nervous as the cross-border operations got under way—
they realized that if things went wrong during the
operation, their actions could mean life or death for the
men in the field.

The pilots of the eight helicopters watched as
familiar terrain flashed beneath their vibrating craft.
They were all veterans of Shining Brass operations and
they had used this entry point on the Vietnam-Laos
border on several previous infiltration missions.

Of the eight Hueys, four were slicks (troop
transporters). The remaining four were the formidable
Huey B gunships, positively bristling with armament
and definitely not slick in appearance. They were armed
with four .30-caliber machine guns and six 2.75-inch
rockets, and, because of the weight of their armament
and the amount of ammunition they carried, they were
some twenty miles per hour slower than the transporters.
As a result, the slick pilots were forced to fly much

slower than they preferred in order to have the protective firepower of the gunships.

The terrain in southeastern Laos was a mixture of dense jungle forests of bamboo and small open areas of tall elephant grass. The Laotian jungle is only marginally different from any other dense jungle in the world. Three layers of foliage—the tops of the tallest trees, the tops of the intermediate-size trees, and the tall dense shrub on the jungle floor—block out most of the available light to the ground. The area beneath this so-called triple canopy jungle is inhabited by a variety of animals, reptiles, and insects, most of which are fascinating to watch but can turn perfectly nasty when they are hungry, threatened, or disturbed.

The bamboo forests in the Laotian jungle were difficult and dangerous to penetrate, as the bladelike leaves and sharp-spiked limbs on the bushes could cut a man to pieces if any attempt was made to rush through them. In the more open areas, the elephant grass grew to a height of about nine or ten feet and, like the bamboo, its leaves were sharp enough to cut through clothing and human skin. The density of the grass in some regions made it a haven for both wild creatures and the cunning North Vietnamese soldiers, who, like the Japanese jungle fighters in World War II, were quite small in size and slender in build. This gave them a distinct advantage over the average-built American soldier when it came to moving about and fighting in dense jungle, bamboo, and elephant grass.

Of the four slicks being escorted into Laos, only one contained the Special Forces team; the remaining three carried only their pilots and crews and were there simply to deceive the enemy. This was standard procedure on infiltration missions and it proved to be quite successful because, even if the enemy were expecting a raid, it was highly unlikely that they would know which slick contained the reconnaissance team.

When the eight Hueys crossed over the border they were scattered out over a small area of sky in a "loose" formation, but as they approached their landing-zone area the slicks went into trail, or line astern, formation. The gunships then moved into position on either side of the slicks to protect the flanks of the formation, and the attention of all the pilots was then focused on the lead slick.

At this point another coded signal was transmitted to the control center in Da Nang, and, high above the Huey formation, two piston-engined A-1 Skyraider fighter bombers of the Air Commando were alerted. The A-1s, or "flying dump trucks," had been circling in a staging area in preparation for the mission. On receipt of the alert signal from the control center, the A-1s left their staging area and moved down to an area much closer to the infiltration point.

As the lead slick approached the landing-zone area the pilot heard the A-1s call that they were on station nearby. That made him feel a little happier, as he was acutely aware of the support the Air Commando aircraft could give if things went wrong. Moments later he spotted a small clear area just ahead and to the right. He called to the slicks behind him that he was going down and immediately started to lower the pitch lever. The helicopter started to sink in response to the downward movement of the pitch lever and the pilot carefully maneuvered his machine into the opening. As he brought his craft to a hover a few feet above the ground, he held his breath in anticipation of enemy fire. He looked through the window above his head and saw the remaining slicks, still in trail formation, pass straight over as if nothing had happened.

When the last slick had passed, he pulled steadily up on the pitch lever and quickly climbed up into formation behind it; all four craft were now in trail again. Shortly afterward, the slick that was now leading the formation suddenly dropped into a clearing, hovered until the remainder of the flight had passed over him, then lifted off and quickly climbed up to the rear of the trail formation.

This little game of leapfrog continued for a considerable period of time and over a fairly wide area. It was performed with such smoothness and efficiency that the slick that dropped down to hover always came back up just in time to take up position right behind the last helicopter. There was obviously only one break in the routine: at a specified point in the game of helicopter leapfrog, a fully armed, nine-man Special Forces team, led by Sergeant Fred Zabitosky, jumped out of one of the helicopters and disappeared into the undergrowth.

If the enemy were in the area they would immediately suspect that an infiltration had taken place, but they could not be sure because decoy infiltrations were often performed to force the North Vietnamese into searching for a phantom team. Even if the enemy were certain that an infiltration was in progress, it was extremely difficult for them to figure out where it had actually taken place because the leapfrogging procedure was always performed over a wide area.

Sergeant Zabitosky's team was made up of a few American Special Forces noncommissioned officers but the majority of the team were the famous Special Forces Nung soldiers. The Nungs were members of a tribe that originated in North Vietnam close to the Chinese border, and a considerable number of them had fled to South Vietnam between 1946 and 1955. They were extremely anti-Communist, and a complete division of Nung soldiers served with distinction under the French government and the government of President Ngo Dinh Diem, which followed the French departure. When the division was demobilized by the

South Vietnamese government, the Nungs made no attempt to return to their homelands in the north and settled in various places in the south.

During the early days of American involvement in Vietnam they were employed by both the Central Intelligence Agency and the Special Forces, which found them to be intelligent, fiercely loyal, and excellent soldiers. They were originally hired as personal body-guards for the Special Forces operating in the remote villages and hamlets of South Vietnam, and they were paid considerably more than members of the regular South Vietnamese Army. Any Special Forces soldier who operated with the Nungs, either in Vietnam, Cambodia, or Laos, will confirm that they were worth every cent they were paid, not only for their fighting ability but for their loyalty.

However, a few problems arose when it became obvious that their loyalty was clearly directed more toward the Americans than to the Vietnamese people or the Vietnamese Army. Unfortunately, the Nungs were to become something of a source of controversy and embarrassment to the South Vietnamese government because of inaccurate reporting by American newspaper and television reporters who labeled them as Special Forces mercenaries. The media likened them to the Gurkha soldiers of the British Army, who are truly mercenary—they fight for the British everywhere in the world except their own homeland of Nepal.

The Nungs, however, were fighting in their own country in a civil war and in no way could they be classed mercenaries. Sadly, the American media, aided gleefully by the Communist propaganda corps, seemed determined not to print the truth about the Nungs, who were truly a very honorable race simply fighting for freedom in their own land.

The Nungs of Sergeant Zabitosky's reconnaissance patrol were experienced guerrilla fighters. Several of them had led somewhat charmed lives as they had seen service with the French Army and had been fighting against the Communist guerrillas for almost fifteen years. The American members of the team were also experienced, particularly Zabitosky, who was on his fourteenth cross-border patrol and his third tour of duty in Vietnam. Shortly after his team left the landing zone, his experience became obvious when they encountered a large force of regular North Vietnamese Army soldiers. When the first shots were fired, the sergeant suspected that they had made contact with at least a regiment of enemy soldiers. He quickly organized his team into a small defense position. He had just positioned his last man when the enemy attacked in force.

The first assault confirmed his suspicions about the size of the enemy group; it was at least a regiment, and Zabitosky's team would need help. The first wave of enemy were driven back by the team's accurate and concentrated fire, but Zabitosky knew that the first assault was just a preliminary move on the part of the enemy to determine what kind of resistance they were facing.

The second major assault would be well organized, and the reconnaissance team would need some help. As the enemy pulled back to regroup, Zabitosky called the Air Commando in their A-1 dump trucks and informed them of the situation. The pilots of the two aircraft were eager to assist and had plenty of ordnance to work with. Zabitosky gave the pilots instructions quickly and concisely—he knew from experience approximately how much time the enemy would take before they mounted another assault.

The pilots quickly confirmed that they understood his request, and Zabitosky, with his team giving him protective fire, crawled forward to the area from which he was certain the enemy would approach. He located a suitable spot and carefully set up an electrically operated M-18 antipersonnel mine, commonly known as a Claymore mine. He attached two white phosphorous grenades to the top of the mine and crawled back to his defense position, carefully feeding out the detonating wire.

The North Vietnamese charged just where the sergeant had expected them to. When they were well within range of the Claymore, he warned his men to keep their heads down, removed the safety bail from the firing device, and detonated the mine. The team heard the familiar cracking blast of the Claymore mixed with the screaming sound that was produced when the seven hundred steel balls encased in the mine were hurled out in a deadly swath.

When the team looked up, they saw a gap in the ranks of the charging enemy that was strewn with victims of the deadly Claymore. A billowing cloud of white smoke from the phosphorous grenades was rising lazily into the sky as hordes of screaming North Vietnamese charged toward them. As the Special Forces team started firing into the enemy ranks, they hoped the Air Commandos would not delay.

When the Skyraider pilots saw the smoke, the lead aircraft swung around and lined his craft up in the direction Zabitosky had called. The second aircraft did likewise, but the pilot throttled back to allow the leader to get well ahead, since he did not wish to be close enough to get caught by the blast of the first series of bombs.

As the first Air Commando bore down on the target, he warned Zabitosky, who immediately yelled to his men to get down. The aircraft roared through and the bombs plummeted down.

When they hit the ground they exploded with a dull thud followed instantly by the great *whooshing* noise that is the unmistakable signature of napalm.

A ragged wall of vivid orange flame erupted, wiping out the first wave of the enemy assault and scorching everything in its path. A strange wind suddenly developed as the bombs' mixture of naphthalene, coconut-palm oil, and gasoline burned fiercely and rapidly consumed hundreds of thousands of cubic feet of oxygen from the air. A furnacelike blast of heat swept across the jungle, and the Special Forces team momentarily felt their breath taken away.

A pall of black smoke was rising in the air as the second aircraft unloaded another ton of napalm with incredible accuracy. When the flames subsided, the reconnaissance team saw that the enemy were in disarray and were retreating. Although the assault had been broken by the awesome napalm bombs and the accuracy of the reconnaissance team's fire, Zabitosky knew that the enemy were not finished but had simply withdrawn to regroup. He moved out from his defense position again and set up another Claymore with a pair of phosphorous grenades.

He had barely returned to his team when the next assault started, but this time the enemy were not quite as obliging as they had been on the previous assault—their line of assault was slightly to one side of the deadly Claymore. Zabitosky solved the problem by exposing himself and opening fire with his automatic rifle. The enemy promptly responded by returning his fire, and they automatically started to converge toward him, just as he had hoped they would.

Once again the deadly M-18 Claymore emitted its cracklike explosion and spewed out the deadly swath of steel balls. The Air Commando pilots saw the trail of white phosphorous smoke and immediately swung their craft down into another bomb run. The enemy assault formation suggested that they were expecting more napalm, and they were obviously surprised when the

Skyraiders showered them with several tons of high-explosive bombs.

The assault was again beaten off, but Zabitosky realized that his team could not hold on much longer against such a superior force. He ordered his team to move quickly back toward the landing zone and called for extraction helicopters. The control center informed him that he would have to wait; there were no helicopters immediately available. However, they did promise him that another pair of Air Commando Skyraiders were approaching the area to relieve the first pair when they ran out of ordnance and ammunition.

Zabitosky arranged his men in a defense circle around the landing zone and waited for the inevitable. He knew that the casualties inflicted against the North Vietnamese by both his small team and the Air Commando Skyraiders were high, and that the enemy would now be more determined than ever to annihilate his tiny group.

The first assault on the lnding zone was beaten off by the snarling-engined Skyraiders and their high-explosive bombs. The second assault was met by the same pair of Skyraiders, now out of bombs and using their machine guns on a strafing run. They were skillfully directed by Zabitosky, who brought them as close as he dared to his own position, and the enemy attack was broken up.

However, the enemy tactics had changed somewhat, as not all of them withdrew under the withering fire of the Skyraiders. Many who survived the strafing run took cover close to the defense circle and started to crawl toward the team. They were well aware of the fact that the aircraft would not come too close to the Special Forces team, and a deadly game of cat-and-mouse developed. It was a game that Zabitosky's men were good at; every enemy soldier who got close to the landing zone paid for it with his life.

An enemy mortar opened up from somewhere in the jungle, but before it could get the range, a Skyraider silenced it with a barrage of screaming rockets. A second and a third mortar were dealt with in a similar manner, and the enemy then returned to their full-scale attacks and attempted infiltration. Within a few hours, a total of twenty-two savage assaults had been beaten back by the deadly Skyraiders and the Special Forces team, and throughout the entire period Zabitosky moved around his defense circle checking on his men, encouraging them, and supplying them spare ammunition.

Just before the twenty-second assault, the control center informed Zabitosky that an extraction team was on the way. When the enemy were once again driven off, he checked on his team members and performed a body count for the statisticians. The nine-man Special Forces team was still intact, but within the close confines of the landing zone there were 109 enemy dead.

The familiar *whapping* sound of the Hueys was heard as the extraction fleet approached, and the enemy mounted one last vicious assault in a desperate attempt to destroy their tormentors. The escorting gunships unleashed a hail of protective fire into the charging enemy as the first slick touched down. Zabitosky sent four of his men to it while he, three Nungs, and one American fought off a close-quarter attack at one side of the landing zone.

The enemy were driven back just as the second slick landed, and Zabitosky sent the remainder of his team racing toward it. Zabitosky was scrambling to get in the door as the Huey pilot "pulled pitch" and lifted off. When they were some seventy-five feet above the ground, the craft was hit with a Soviet-made rocket grenade and Zabitosky was blown out the door.

When he recovered consciousness he was lying on the landing zone, with the crashed and burning helicopter lying some twenty feet away from him. The

gunships were still whirling around the perimeter laying
down a barrage of fire, but he could hear enemy
bullets whining over his head, and some were striking
the ground beside him. He could see the pilot and
the copilot still sitting in the burning Huey. As he
dragged himself to his feet, his chest and back felt as
though they had been jumped on by half an Airborne
division.

Zabitosky scrambled over to the helicopter and
dragged the pilot—who was alive but badly dazed—out
of his seat and away from the wreck. Then he ran back
and started to pull out the copilot, but just as he got his
arms around the man, the helicopter's fuel cells exploded and threw them both clear of the wreck.

As he picked himself up off the ground, Zabitosky
saw another slick land nearby. He now realized that,
apart from his aching back and chest, he was also
burned, but he paid no attention to it and picked up
the bulky copilot, slung him over his shoulder, and
started toward the dazed pilot.

The crew chief of the waiting slick was about to
leave the helicopter to come to his assistance when a
group of enemy burst onto the landing zone. He swung
his machine gun around and drove them back as Zabitosky
picked up the dazed pilot and scrambled toward the
helicopter, where the crew chief quickly dragged all
three of them inside and immediately returned to his
gun to drive off another group of enemy. The pilot
pulled pitch, quickly cleared the area, and headed for
the nearest field hospital in Vietnam.

As the rescue helicopters made their way back into
South Vietnam, the Air Commando Skyraiders destroyed
what remained of the crashed and burning helicopter.
They also bombed and strafed the remaining enemy
with total impunity, as they did not have to concern
themselves with avoiding their own ground forces.

*   *   *

Despite Zabitosky's valiant efforts, the copilot died of his wounds, but the pilot was back in action shortly after the crash. Zabitosky discovered that, apart from his burns, he had crushed ribs and vertebrae, and he was pulled out of action.

On March 7, 1969, Sergeant First Class Fred Zabitosky, for actions that were above and beyond the call of duty, became the fifth member of the United States Army Special Forces to receive the nation's highest award for bravery—the Medal of Honor.

11

AFTER-ACTION REPORTS

After-action reports are mandatory at the conclusion of any operation involving United States Armed Forces. They are usually filed by the unit or company commander, regardless of rank; in the event that the officer commanding the force is lost during an operation, the report is then completed by the most senior surviving member, or by an officer appointed to the task.

There is a format for after-action reports that requires that they be brief and concise and that they stick to the pertinent details of the sequence of events. The first part of the report must be a chronological order of events, and the second part a brief account of the action with appropriate comments. When the report is submitted, unit commanders are free to add, in their own words, any additional information that they consider useful for the purposes of clarity and enlightenment. But this is not often done, since most commanders are content simply to submit the required format.

Special Forces after-action reports are invariably classified, as they often contain details of tactics, equipment, and other information that could jeopardize our national security. Such classified reports are reviewed periodically by a military security review board; if they feel that the information contained in a report is "out of date" and no longer "sensitive," the report is declassified and readership is no longer restricted.

The following example of a Special Forces afteraction report is declassified. The first part of the report is the traditional and terse chronological order of events. The second part—the account of the action and general remarks—is somewhat less terse and allows a bit better insight into the situation during the foray.

The report covers the period from November 1 through 7, 1966, and is an account of a special operation that was code-named "Attleboro." This was the first phase of the operation, and the report deals with the actions of the Special Forces Mike Force (Mobile Strike Force) assigned to the III Corps region of South Vietnam. For military purposes South Vietnam was divided into four Corps areas, I, II, III, and IV, starting at the demilitarized zone in the north of the country with I Corps, and finishing in the southernmost part with IV Corps. In 1966 the area identified as III Corps started just below Saigon and stretched northward, covering an area of approximately ten thousand square miles.

All military reports are highly abbreviated and are almost unintelligible if the jargon is not known. Therefore, in the examples that follow, everything in parenthesis has been added by the author for ease of understanding; otherwise, the report is transcribed almost exactly as it was when it was first submitted in November 1966. (Unfortunately, none of the maps mentioned are available.)

SUBJECT: after action Report MIKE Force/"Attleboro" 1–7 Nov 66. General: a. Third Corps MIKE Force had moved to Loc Ninh on 30 October 1966 in support of moving to new camp site, and was on an operation in Loc Ninh area.

b. Third Corps MIKE Force was alerted 2 November

1966 to move from Loc Ninh to Suoi Da. The move was completed at 1430 (hours) 2 November 1966.

Task Organization
    a. 530 Nungs in three companies
    b. Seven USASF EM (Army Special Forces enlisted men)
    c. One USASF Officer

Mission: Combat Reconnaissance
    Sequence of Events:
    1 Nov 2210—China Boy (code name for MIKE
        Force) alerted for movement from Loc Ninh to
        Suoi Da.
    2 Nov 0800—1st MIKE Force company extracted
        from LZ (landing zone).
    0900—Company closed Loc Ninh.
    1045—2nd Company extraction began.
    1215—Completed extraction 2nd company.
    1230—C-123 aircraft began arriving Loc Ninh.
        Direct support helicopter company moved
        from Loc Ninh to Tay Ninh East to lift MF
        (MIKE Force) from Tay Ninh East; and to lift
        MF from Tay Ninh West to Suoi Da.
    1352—Tay Ninh.
    1530—Movement of MF from Tay Ninh to Suoi
        Da completed.
    2 Nov 1630—China Boy Company 3 deployed.
    3 Nov 0830—China Boy Company 1 deployed.
    1220—China Boy Company 3 engaged est VC
        Co vic XT 486687 (estimated Viet Cong
        company; *vic* means vicinity and XT486687
        is the map grid reference approximation),
        VC broke contact 1245, fled north. SSG (Staff
        Sergeant) Monaghan wounded right arm and
        fingers GSW (gun shot wound).
    1815—China Boy Company 1 made contact vic

XT458587 with est VC platoon. VC broke contact at 1830. SSG Garza WIA (wounded in action) GSW.

4 Nov 0730—China Boy Company 1 hit mined area vic XT561588. One MF KIA (killed in action), two MF WIA. Med Evac chopper downed by fire vic XT485622, while en route to China Boy Company 1's location. One U.S. crew member KIA (killed in action), chopper was recovered.

1445—China Boy Company 3 made contact vic XT416670 with est VC Bn or Regt (battalion or regiment). China Boy Company 3 withdrew south and called in airstrike. On initial contact, chain saws, generators, and trucks could be heard. VC counterfired with 81mm and 60mm mortars, AW and SA fire (automatic weapon and small arms), then tried to close with Company 3 elements.

1800—Received resupply of ammunition and food vic XT435668.

2200—China Boy Company 3 indicated that he was receiving heavy casualties and VC were encircling him.

2300—China Boy 3 indicated light contact.

5 Nov 0230—China Boy 3 indicates contact with VC has ceased.

0730—China Boy 3 receiving heavy volume of fire. Requested reinforcements.

0745—Radio contact with China Boy Company 3 broken.

0800—China Boy Companies 1 and 2 proceeding to China Boy Company 3's location.

0845—China Boy Company 2 hit VC bunkers. Negative contact.

0940—28 MF personnel picked up by CIDG CO from Suoi Da (Civilian Irregular Defense Group Company).

0945—China Boy Company 3 having casualties
evacuated vic XT388634.

1200—Three USSF MIA. (USSF: United States
Special Forces, not necessarily Army Special Forces, as there were other U.S. personnel who came under the general title of
"Special," i.e. SEALs, etc.)

55 MF from China Boy 3 made linkup with
China Boy 1 and 2. Of those, 15 to 25 WIA.

1330—One MF drowned while crossing river
with China Boy Company 1.

6 Nov 1040—Est VC platoon with mortars attacked
Suoi Da airfield, 4 CIDG (Civilian Irregular
Defense Group) KIA, 2 WIA.

1700—9 MF personnel closed in to Suoi Da.

7 Nov 1430—MF begins move to Loc Ninh.

1600—MF completes move to Loc Ninh.

1645—One U.S. body found.

1830—MF bodies returned to Bien Hoa by air.

On 30 October, all 3 companies of the Mike Force
deployed to Loc Ninh, A-331, Binh Long province (a
Special Forces Detachment, designated A-331, was based
at Loc Ninh), to conduct operations in response to
intelligence reports that the camp was a possible target
for a major VC attack prior to 11 November 1966.
However, hard intelligence reports received on 1
November indicated that a VC regiment had moved
into the operational area of Camp Suoi Da, A-322, Tay
Ninh province.

A decision was made to move the Mike Force into
that area, and this was accomplished on 2 November.
On 031222 November (November 3 at 1222 hrs), the
3rd Mike Force Company made contact with an estimated VC company. The VC immediately broke contact
and an airstrike was called in on their route of withdrawal. At 031845, contact was again established with

an estimated VC platoon which resulted in 10 VC KIA and two USASF WIA.

At 040730, the 1st Mike Force Company hit a mined area and suffered one KIA and two WIA. A Med Evac chopper in the same general vicinity was shot down by small arms fire and resulted in one US KIA. At 041445, the 3rd Mike Force Company made contact with an estimated battalion or regimental-sized VC force. This contact resulted in 15 VC KIA and two Mike Force WIA. The Mike Force Company was still in contact at 041540 and attempted to withdraw to the south.

At 042000 the Mike Force Commander reported that he was surrounded and had 35 casualties, KIA. The remaining two CIDG companies departed Camp Suoi Da to reinforce the operation. At 042305, the 3rd Mike Force Company Commander reported that he was still in contact. Enemy casualties reported at this time were 50 VC KIA. Contact with the VC was broken at 050330. At 050900, the 3rd Mike Force Company again reported that they were receiving a heavy volume of fire. They were instructed to secure a LZ (landing zone) so that an attempt could be made to extract them from the area. This was accomplished at 051200. All Mike Force elements were extracted at 051830.

Interview with SFC E7 Heaps (Sergeant First Class, grade 7), 7 Nov 66. 3rd Field Hospital.

At 021630 Nov China Boy 3 landed at LZ vicinity XT491644 and began moving north. At 031220 Nov, vic XT473683, China Boy discovered tunnel complex, VC fired on China Boy wounding SSG Monaghan. China Boy withdrew east to LZ vic XT487686. Med Evac arrived, casualties were loaded, but because chopper was overloaded it could not take off. SSG Hunt, who came in with the Med Evac, elected to remain with China Boy 3 so that casualties could be evacuated.

Again China 3 moved west to tunnel complex, but could not take it because of intense fire. China Boy 3 broke contact and moved to vic XT464692. Here they heard several motors that sounded like generators and trucks, plus several chain saws. Heavy contact was made. China Boy 3 received heavy automatic weapons fire and mortar fire. Mortars sounded like 60mm. China Boy 3 broke contact and moved to LZ vic XT435667. All during the time they were moving to LZ they were receiving sporadic small arms fire. Also when they crossed road vic XT453667, they received mortar fire.

At LZ vic XT435667 China Boy 3 received resupply of food and ammunition. From resupply LZ the unit moved to vic XT444672, went into defensive perimeter and began breaking down ammo. While they were breaking down ammo, the VC attacked from the east in a U-shaped formation. It was beginning to get dark and the VC withdrew to approximately 100 meters east of China Boy 3's position and maintained contact all night. At approximately 0645–0700 the following morning the VC made another assault on China Boy 3's position and overran them. SFC Heaps and SSG Hunt were wounded during this assault. SFC Heaps said he was knocked unconscious and when he came to SSG Hunt was giving him first aid. Heaps and Hunt decided to get to the LZ vic XT424680. They had two Mike Force with them, one was wounded. They couldn't move very fast or very far without resting, and Heaps and Hunt would pass out periodically. Finally Hunt said he could go no further so Heaps left one Mike Force with Hunt and continued to the LZ. After this Heaps didn't remember anything.

REFERENCE: LOC NINH Map Sheet 6245 II
         465691 to 473681, first contact.

Area of operations: Major contact overrun at 440669.

* * *

Weather: Excellent, high clouds, temperature.

Terrain: Jungle, thick, close to water supply, within 500 meters of road on high ground.

Fortifications: Tunnel and bunker complexes for one, two, or squad-size positions. All with overhead cover and prearranged fields of fire. Positions were hardened against direct fire.

Weapons, uniforms and equipment: Automatic weapons were in abundance; the two weapons captured were AKs. They had a lot of machine guns, sounded like .30 cal, heavy. Uniforms were mixed, personnel KIA had on black shoes. All of the soldiers encountered had complete sets of web gear.

Significant weapons: Grenade launcher which looked like our "IAW" (Infantry Antitank Weapon—M72A1-M72A2 LAAW), light in weight, approximately three feet long, markings appeared to be Chinese, possible identification: Chinese antitank grenade type launcher type 56, page 155, DA (Department of the Army) pamphlet 381-10. Indirect fire was provided by 60mm mortars, identification by rounds.

Tactics: Fire discipline was excellent. Upon making contact, VC fired in mass: upon breaking contact VC ceased fire without sporadic firing. The VC maintained contact while the unit was trying to break contact. They mortared and sniped at them in the retreat. After fixing the new location of the 3rd Company, the VC attacked using squad fire and maneuver up to grenade range and then reverted to individual action. By this time it was almost dark, so the VC withdrew approximately 100 meters and maintained contact all night. At 0645-0700 the next morning they assaulted using the same tactics with a heavy volume of fire suppressing the 3rd Company's position.

Movement was forward by flanks and frontal assault forces.

Other: The VC troopers were young and aggressive. At grid 465691—generators and chain saws were heard.

The last page on a report such as this would contain the casualty figures of both sides, both by body count and by estimation, and would also specify all units involved in the action.

Roll of Honor

In the seven-year period from July 1964, to August 1971, Army Special Forces soldiers earned a total of seventeen Medals of Honor, eight of which were awarded posthumously. The list that follows is in the order of the dates of the action and not the dates of the actual awards. However, the rank indicated is the individual's rank at the time of the award.

1. Captain Roger Hugh C. Donlon
2. Captain Charles Q Williams (died in 1982)
3. First Lieutenant George K. Sisler (posthumous)
4. Master Sergeant Charles E. Hoskins, Jr. (posthumous)
5. Sergeant Gordon Yntema (posthumous)
6. Captain Drew D. Dix
7. Sergeant First Class Eugene Ashley, Jr. (posthumous)
8. Sergeant First Class Fred W. Zabitosky
9. Master Sergeant Roy Benavidez (award presented by President Ronald Reagan, February 1981)
10. Specialist Five John Kedenburg (posthumous)
11. Sergeant First Class William M. Bryant (posthumous)
12. Staff Sergeant Franklin D. Miller
13. Sergeant Gary B. Beikirch
14. Sergeant Brian L. Buker (posthumous)
15. Captain Robert L. Howard

16. Sergeant John R. Cavaiani
17. First Lieutenant Loren D. Hagen (posthumous)

Soldiers of the Special Forces have also earned the following numbers of awards during their operations in Southeast Asia:

Distinguished Service Cross	60
Silver Star	814
Bronze Star	10,160
Purple Heart	2,658
Distinguished Service Medal	1
Legion of Merit Award	235
Distinguished Flying Cross	46
Soldier's Medal	232
Bronze Star with V Device	3,074
Air Medal with V Device	394
Air Medal	4,527
Army Commendation Medal with V Device	1,258
Army Commendation Medal	5,650

In addition to these individual awards, the following Unit Awards were also earned:

Two Presidential Unit Citations (one through the Navy); Meritorious Unit Citation; Vietnam Cross of Gallantry with Palm; Valorous Unit Award; Vietnam Civic Action Award; and the Navy Unit Commendation Ribbon.

Finally, the United States Army Special Forces were credited with participation in twelve campaigns, and those members involved are permitted to wear the appropriate campaign ribbons.

The Fighting Elite ™

AMERICA'S GREAT MILITARY UNITS

by Ian Padden

Here is the magnificent new series that brings you into the world of America's most courageous and spectacular combat forces—the Fighting Elite. Each book is an exciting account of a particular military unit—its origins and training programs, its weaponry and deployment—and lets you relive its most famous battles in tales of war and valor that will live forever. All the books include a special 8-page photo insert.

BANTAM
SHOP·AT·HOME
C·A·T·A·L·O·G

Special Offer
Buy a Bantam Book
for only 50¢.

Now you can have an up-to-date listing of Bantam's hundreds of titles plus take advantage of our unique and exciting bonus book offer. A special offer which gives you the opportunity to purchase a Bantam book for only 50¢. Here's how!

By ordering any five books at the regular price per order, you can also choose any other single book listed (up to a $4.95 value) for just 50¢. Some restrictions do apply, but for further details why not send for Bantam's listing of titles today!

Just send us your name and address and we will send you a catalog!
